India and Pakistan's Nuclear Weapons Capability 2019

SAGHIR IQBAL

DEDICATION

I dedicate this book to all those who gave me encouragement, support and guidance. Foremost, to my father (late) Raja Mohammed Iqbal and to my mother Azra Begum, from whom I have learnt so much.

CONTENTS

ACKNOWLEDGMENTS

I am very grateful to a host of people for their various contributions towards this book. I am particularly very grateful to Professor Syed Peerzada Mahmud Shah Bookhari who deserves much commendation for his constant encouragement and support throughout the hard times of the programme.

India and Pakistan's Nuclear Weapons Capability
2019

Pakistani Army Strategic Arsenal

Abstract

As the largest country in South Asia, India has continued to set the tone and define the parameters of inter-state relations within its region. Since 1971, this has involved it openly seeking short-term regional pre-eminence, as well as global power projection in the long-term. Encouraged by its size, the commitment of its people and by the huge military machine and its disposal, Delhi has consistently sought to conduct relations with its South Asian neighbours on its own terms. In the process, successive Indian governments have candidly deployed policy tools ranging from interventions to annexation and from subversions to economic blockades, to promote India's own policy goals (Sikkim 1970, troops into Sri Lanka in 1987 and in Maldives in 1988, and the economic blockade of Nepal 1989).[1]

This assertive role has caused considerable tension with Pakistan. In November 1986, India launched its largest military exercise ever, Operation Brass Tacks, close to the Pakistan border. The Pakistan Army responded with threatening counter-movements, raising serious concern that war might break out. An India-Pakistan hot line was set up after this. In May 1990, the uprising in Kashmir again brought the armies of Pakistan and India very close to conflict.[2] Tensions have continued due to the heavy

[1] Malik, op cit:153

handed and brutal tactics that India has done to the Kashmiri people in Indian occupied Kashmir. The Kashmiri separatist/freedom fighter, Burhan Wani's death on July 9, 2016 has sparked mass protests, with over 50,000 people congregated to mourn his death and joined his funeral procession.[3] With Indian development of Cold Start Doctrine (CSD) and a hawkish government – serious border firing has led to extreme tensions, that has a potential to breakout into an all-out war with nuclear Pakistan.

The Hindu fundamentalist Bharatiya Janata Party (BJP) - led coalition government in India has continued with the development of nuclear weapons to further her hegemonic goals in the area. This was reflected in the three nuclear devices exploded on May 11, 1998 and another two on May 13, 1998 at Pokhran, in spite of general opposition to testing.[4]

Pakistan viewed India's post-nuclear test statements as intimidatory and threatening to its security. The change in the regional balance was immediately obvious, and despite calls for restraint, the global response to India's tests and the promise of military aid from the US were seen as insufficient commitments to protect Pakistan's security. Pakistan has always seen itself as a bulwark to India's regional hegemonistic aspirations, and thus decided to conduct nuclear tests of its own, on 28th May 1998. The Indian tests had come after the BJP party came into government two months earlier, on the strength of a mandate which made an Indian nuclear capability as a top priority if elected.[5]

The BJP appeared to base its approach on two assumptions- Pakistan's acceptance of India's regional hegemony if it was unable to match the nuclear tests; and the fragility of Pakistan's economy, which would be unable to bear an arms race even if it did have a nuclear capability. Either way, at least Pakistan would be faced to come out into the open about its nuclear status, with either result impacting on Pakistan's regional status.[6] This book looks at both countries nuclear weapons capability and the impact this has on the region.

[2] Ibid

[3] Who Was Burhan Wani? And Why Is Kashmir Mourning Him? - https://www.huffingtonpost.in/burhan-wani/who-was-burhan-wani-and-why-is-kashmir-mourning-him_a_21429499/

[4] JDW, India becomes Sixth Nuclear Weapons State, 1998, Pg4
[5] The Daily Telegraph, Nuclear Blasts Puts Pakistan in Arms Race, 1998, Pg1
[6] The Times, Pakistan Blasts into the Arms Race, Times Newspaper Ltd, 1998, Pg1

SAGHIR IQBAL

The Indian Air Force has purchased sophisticated French Rafale multi-role combat aircraft

Abbreviation

ALCM – Air Launched Cruise Missile

AAR - Air to air refuelling

AEW&C – Airborne Early Warning and Control Aircraft

BJP – Bharatiya Janata Party (Hindu Fundamentalist Group)

BM – Ballistic Missiles

BMD – Ballistic Missile defence

CTBT – Comprehensive Test Ban Treaty

GLCM – Ground Launched Cruise Missile

ICBM – Intercontinental Ballistic Missile

IAF – Indian Air Force

JF-17 – Joint Fighter 17 Thunder

MAD – Mutually assured Destruction

MIRV – Multiple Independently Targetable Reentry Vehicle

NPT – Nuclear proliferation Treaty

PAF – Pakistan Air Force

SRBM – Short Range Ballistic Missile

SLCM – Submarine Launched Cruise Missile

SLBM – Submarine Launched Ballistic Missile

WMD – Weapons of Mass Destruction

A pair of armed PAF JF17 Thunder Combat aircraft on a training sortie
(Promotional video) PAF[7]

---

[7] https://www.youtube.com/watch?v=ZthdDd1Qj6A

CHAPTER 1 THE NUCLEAR OPTION AND REGIONAL DETERRENCE

Pakistani military personnel stand beside long-range ballistic Shaheen I missiles during the Pakistan Day military parade in Islamabad

Since the end of the Cold War period, nuclear weapons have been reduced from a massive 70,300 warheads in 1986 to an estimated 14,550 bombs in 2017.[8] In 2017 the following nine countries possessed nuclear weapons and all have been developing a number of methods to launch nuclear weapons to deter any would be adversary (land-based intercontinental ballistic missiles, strategic bombers, and submarine-launched ballistic missiles) - the USA, Russia, UK, France, China, India, Pakistan, Israel and North Korea possess nuclear weapons.[9]

All the nuclear powers have either developed or are in the process of developing different technologies to ensure that they are able to deter a would be adversary. New ballistic missiles, air launched cruise missiles

---

[8] https://fas.org/issues/nuclear-weapons/status-world-nuclear-forces/

[9] https://www.sipri.org/media/press-release/2017/global-nuclear-weapons-modernization-remains-priority

(ALCM), ground (GLCM) and sea based nuclear delivery systems are being pursued by the nuclear powers.[10]

Table 1. World nuclear forces, 2019

Country	Year of first nuclear test	Deployed warheads*	Other warheads	Total 2017
USA	1945	1,800	5,000	6,800
Russia	1949	1,950	5,050	7,000
UK	1952	120	95	215
France	1960	280	20	300
China	1964		270	270
India	1974		140–150	140–150
Pakistan	1998		150–160	150–160
Israel	. .		80	80
North Korea	2006		10-20	10-20
Total		4,150	10,785	14,935

* Deployed warheads refers to warheads placed on missiles or located on bases with operational forces. ** Other warheads refers to warheads that are held in reserve or that are retired and awaiting dismantlement. SIPRI Yearbook 2017.

https://www.sipri.org/media/press-release/2017/global-nuclear-weapons-modernization-remains-priority

---

[10] https://www.armscontrol.org/factsheets/Nuclearweaponswhohaswhat

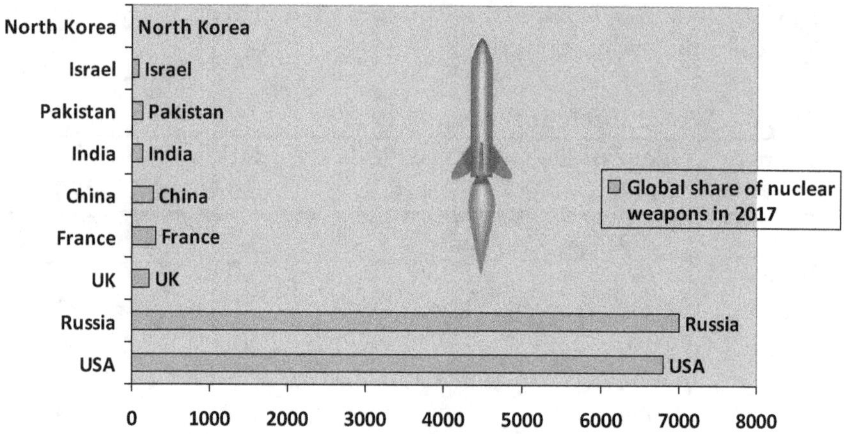

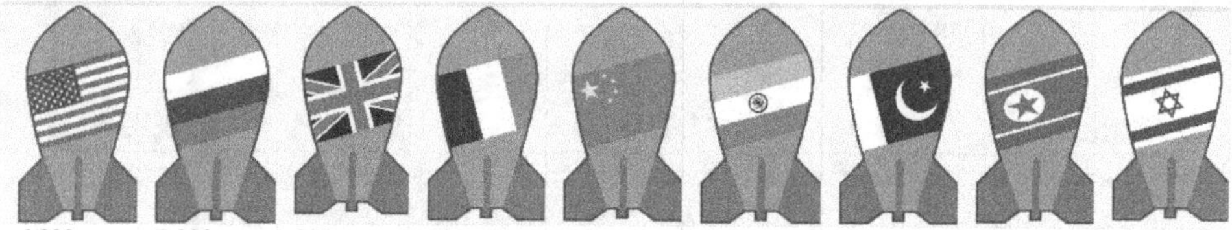

USA	Russia	UK	France	China	India	Pakistan	North Korea	Israel
6,800	7,000	215	300	270	150	160	20	80

https://fas.org/issues/nuclear-weapons/status-world-nuclear-forces/

The Nuclear Option and Regional Deterrence

The principle reason for nuclear and missile proliferation in the Indian sub-continent is the rivalry between India and Pakistan. The security dynamics of the region are complicated further by India's threat perception of China. Pakistan's efforts to develop nuclear delivery systems are intended primarily to counter India's substantial conventional military advantage and its perception of India's nuclear threat.[11]

India started on the road to nuclear autonomy after 1962s border clashes

---

[11] Fareed Zakaria, How to be a Great Cheap, NewsWeek, T.P.L Printers Ltd, May 25, 1998, Pg26

between India and China,[12] which was followed by China going nuclear in 1964.[13] Despite improved relations recently, China is perceived as a long-term threat by India. Secondary to this threat perception is India's ambition to achieve regional hegemony and global prestige. It has long aspired for a permanent seat on the UN Security Council and India's policymakers believed that this was only possible if India was a declared nuclear power.[14]

Pakistan began its nuclear weapons program after losing the 1971 war, accelerating it in response to India's 1974 nuclear test. Pakistan's Prime Minister in 1974, Zulifikar Bhutto, declared that Pakistanis would 'eat grass' rather than surrender the nuclear option.[15] Bhutto believed the nuclear option would give Pakistan a military countermeasure against India's large conventional military, which had been strengthened even further with the possibility of a nuclear device. Like India, Pakistan's nuclear status has become a symbol of national prestige, adding to the average Pakistani citizen's perception that Pakistan was a military match for India at any time.[16]

India Shocks the World

On May 1998, India announced that it had detonated five nuclear devices,[17] under the pretext of a potential security threat. This led to Pakistan testing its own devices within a matter of weeks, in order to 'balance the security of the region'.[18] India also announced a weapons development program, to the chagrin of international opinion. Critics argue that India's decision was devoid of a strategic rationale- it went against India's own 50-year old principles of opposition to nuclear deterrence, and rejection of the proposition that weapons of mass destruction generate security.[19]

Upon inspection, India has failed to justify its reasons for accelerating nuclear proliferation in the region. There has been no deterioration in India's security environment in recent years. On the contrary, India has improved relations with its neighbours, especially China. The Indian drive toward nuclear weapons capability had also not been fuelled by any necessity to check Pakistan. India, with its superior conventional strength, did not need nuclear weapons to counter a then non-nuclear Pakistan. Nor

---

[12] Ibid

[13] Paul Rogers, Guide to Nuclear Weapons 1984-85, C.J.W Printers Ltd, 1984, Pg88

[14] Zakaria op cit:26

[15] Nils Bhinda, The Kashmir Conflict-1990, Earthscan Publication Ltd, 1994, Pg72

[16] Ibid

[17] India Today, India is now a nuclear weapons state, Living India Media Ltd, May 1998, Pg12

[18] India Today, Pakistan's nuclear test, what now, June 1998, Pg14

[19] Ibid

had India been under serious pressure to sign unequal arms control agreements. It seems obvious that the BJP was clearing the ground for India's hegemonic agenda.[20]

Several observers of the South Asian scene have argued that neither China nor Pakistan have posed any increased threat to India, leaving little reason for it to go nuclear. The consensus of opinion is that the Hindu fundamentalist government of Prime Minister Vajpayee was desperate to consolidate the power it had strived for since India's independence. Indeed, their election manifesto had been built around the premise of reviving India's nuclear program.

According to Lawrence Freedman, Professor of War Studies (Kings College), the real reasons for testing its nuclear device was,

"The answer lies in the election of a hawkish Indian government. It has offered the strategic rationale that nuclear weapons are still needed to deter a Chinese threat – despite the apparent relaxation of relations between these two giant countries in recent years – and the need to keep Pakistan in check. More important, however, are questions of national pride. The Indian nuclear debate has always proceeded on the assumption that nuclear status really matters when it comes to setting the international hierarchy".[21]

On Pakistan's reasons for conducting its nuclear device, Freedman said, **"Once India has detonated its weapons, Pakistan really had little choice. It is smaller than India and much weaker, both economically and militarily. It had to prove its own nuclear capacity to reassure its population that India could be deterred".[22]**

He also said, **"Given that neither China nor the U.S could offer Pakistan a nuclear guarantee as an alternative, its options were limited".[23]**

India's BJP government is known for anti-Muslim stance. BJP was responsible for the destruction of the famous 16th century Babri mosque.[24] BJP, before coming to power, vowed to retake Azaad (free) Kashmir from Pakistan.[25] Home Minister L K Advani made a statement that the strategic

---

[20] Eric Arnett, What Threat?, Bulletin of the Atomic Scientists, 1997, Pg53

[21] Lawrence Freedman, National Pride sets the Sabre Rattling, Daily Mail, May 29, 1998, Pg6

[22] Ibid

[23] Ibid

[24] Edward W. Desmond, Unity or Chaos?, Time November 12, 1990, Pg42

scenario in the subcontinent has changed dramatically after the current round of Indian tests. He also did not rule out limited military strikes across the border at insurgency training camps in Pakistan. After the Indian tests, India's Home Minister L K Advani spelt out the Indian intent, He said

"Islamabad should realise the change in the geo-strategic situation in the region and the world and rollback its anti-India policy, especially with regard to Kashmir".[26]

And that **"India's bold and decisive step to become a nuclear-weapon state has brought about a qualitatively new stage in Indo-Pakistan relations, particularly in finding a solution to the Kashmir problem".**[27]

And that it **"signifies India's resolve to deal firmly and strongly with Pakistan's hostile designs and activities in Kashmir",** and that India will now take **'proactive'** measures against Kashmir militancy. Almost as if building a case for a rapid strike Advani referred to the Kashmir separatists as **"foreign mercenaries"**.[28]

In the wake of the Indian tests, the weak and indecisive world reaction to the Pokhran explosions convinced Pakistan of the new threats to its security. The first G-8 gathering did not display a tough will to punish India's unprovoked nuclear delinquency. Russia was all but silent. The non-aligned nations meeting in Colombia did not strongly condemn the Indian tests. Above all, the United States was not prepared to offer Pakistan a security guarantee sufficient to allay its heightened fears. In fact, since 1990 the US has refused to deliver 28 F-16s which Pakistan had bought from America and for which it had already paid $658 million years ago.[29]

This had not only weakened Pakistan's conventional defence capability but had also weakened the countries confidence in Washington as a dependable ally. In the light of these circumstances and after India had carried out its nuclear tests, followed by hostile and proactive statements made against Pakistan by Indian leaders (such as L.K Advani). And considering the likelihood of an Indian attack on Pakistani-held Kashmir, Pakistani forces were reportedly placed on highest alert. Pakistan then chose to respond in kind, by exploding its own nuclear device at Chagai in its Balochistan

---

[25] News International, India will have to reclaim Azaad Kashmir says Defence Minister, Jang Publications, Ltd, 1998, Pg1
[26] News International, Advani's Nuclear Blackmail, August 10, 1998, Pg1
[27] Ibid
[28] Ibid
[29] News International, Advani's Nuclear Blackmail, August 10, 1998, Pg1

province on May 28 and 30.[30]

Once the nuclear capability had been demonstrated, Pakistan achieved strategic parity with India. Indeed, as Indian critics of the BJP's decision pointed out, the Indian test conferred several benefits upon Pakistan: it enabled Pakistan to conduct nuclear tests openly, virtually eliminated India's military edge in conventional weapons, and brought the Kashmir dispute, which was the main cause of Indo-Pakistan tensions, in the global spotlight.[31]

The rise of Hindu fundamentalism

In fact, domestic considerations, not external threats or dissatisfaction with the way the nuclear weapon states have acted, are paramount. One cannot comprehend why India crossed the nuclear threshold without giving decisive weight to the changing self-perceptions of the Indian elite and the profound transformations the country has undergone in the last 10 years with the rise of a viciously sectarian, and deeply belligerent political force, the Bharatiya Janata Party (BJP) and its affiliates.[32]

The BJP, a right-wing reactionary political party established in 1980, propounds an ideology of aggressive anti-Muslim, anti-secular Hindu nationalism. It has made dramatic gains in the past decade: In 1984 the BJP had only two seats in the 543- member Lower House of Parliament; today it is the single largest party with 180 seats, and it heads a coalition government.[33]

Behind the BJP and inseparable from it-is the Rashtriya Swayamsevak Sangh (National Volunteer Corps), which is the real head of an overall combine, called the Bajrang Dal, a huge anti-Muslim cultural force that operates the Vishwa Hindu Parishad (World Hindu Council). The Rashtriya Swayamsevak Sangh (RSS) has fascist characteristics. The RSS does not contest parliamentary elections nor does it hold elections to various organizational posts. It is a secret, all-male organization whose objective is to establish a Hindu state.[34]

The rise of Hindu nationalism has completely altered the discourse of Indian politics and it is beginning to transform the character of Indian society. Nothing else so fully explains why India took the decision to shed its nuclear ambiguity. India's nuclearization reflects the belief of the BJP-

---

[30] India Today, Bang for Bang, June 1998, Pg10
[31] Zakaria op cit:26
[32] Hewitt, op cit:182
[33] Ibid
[34] Ibid

RSS as well as growing sections of the Indian elite that nuclear weapons constitute a shortcut to establishing the country's stature as a major actor-in Prime Minister Atal Bihari Vajpayee's words, the nuclear tests "show our strength and silence our enemies".[35]

From the BJP, nuclear weapons are an article of faith, part of the essential identity of a powerful awe-inspiring, militarist Hindu India that can boast of its manliness and virility and thus prove to the world the superiority of Hindu 'civilization'. [36]

<u>Nuclear Deterrence</u>

India-China relations, which had greatly improved in the 1990s with the signing of two major peace agreements in 1991 and 1996, have received a decisive setback, because of India's testing of its nuclear device and the hostile remarks made by Indian ministers. China will now see India as a nuclear rival and act accordingly. India has already declared that its missile development program is meant to create a deterrent against China. India suspects China of being the country most likely to challenge its efforts to emerge as a regional power.[37]

Pakistani leaders believe that a nuclear capability is essential to deter war with India, or failing that, to ensure the survival of the nation. Its nuclear program has widespread political and popular support. Missile procurement and development, initially to counter the Indian missile program which began in the mid-1980s, are driven by a desire to augment limited offensive air capabilities against India (which holds almost 2:1 advantage in combat aircraft) and to field a more effective delivery system.[38]

Most Pakistani strategies and military leaders regard the nuclear choice as a prudent strategic bargain. As Pakistan's former Army Chief of Staff, General Mirza Aslam Beg, noted a nuclear deterrent for Pakistan represents "the cheapest option for peace",[39] balancing Indians and Pakistanis see nuclear weapons as an instrument of independence from the United States and other outside powers.

Neither India nor Pakistan regards the current international non-proliferation regime (the NPT) as relevant or helpful to its security problems. India has always regarded the NPT as the centrepiece of a

---

[35] Sunday Telegraph, India celebrates its Nuclear dream, May 1998, Pg27
[36] Ibid
[37] Arnett op cit:153
[38] News International, Armed to the Teeth, 1998, Pg27
[39] Ibid

conscious U.S. policy of denying lesser nations access in the fruits of economic and industrial development, to which the world's largest democracy should be entitled. Pakistan has offered to sign the NPT if India does it as well.[40]

However, both sides should take a deep breath and consider the historical lesson of 1962, when the United States and the Soviet Union moved to the brink of nuclear war over Cuba. We now know something we did not know then. Had President Kennedy ordered the invasion of Cuba, Russian commanders in Cuba were under orders from Premier Khruschev to launch nuclear missiles against the United States.[41]

Kashmir in today's Cuba. India and Pakistan are poised to fight over Kashmir, only now they have nuclear weapons to back up their passionate claims to this disputed territory. A miscalculation by either side could result in the unthinkable calamity that the United States and Russia barely avoided in 1962. The consequences of a nuclear war between India and Pakistan would be catastrophic.[42]

Nuclear stockpiles

India has conducted only one nuclear test (1974) until recently, and has conducted five nuclear tests in May 1998. Since the 1974 test, India is believed to have produced some 130 nuclear devices and made significant progress in refining its bomb-making technology.[43] Pakistan has sufficient materials to arm a 140 nuclear weapons.[44]

Nuclear command-and-control

Both India and Pakistan have civilian governments led by a prime-minister. The process of consultation used to arrive at a decision to test nuclear weapons was obviously highly motivated by a small circle in the ruling parties, with the decision taken quickly without public discussions. The decision to use nuclear weapons would undoubtedly be a far more searching and deliberate one.[45] The former Indian Defence Minister George Fernandes told Jane's Defence Weekly that the country is working toward a nuclear command and control system under the exclusive control of a national security council, which is being formed.[46] In Pakistan, where the

---

[40] Ibid
[41] J.A.S Greenville, History of the World, HarperCollins Publishers, 1994, Pg593
[42] Ibid
[43] JDW, Trials provide Data for ranges of weapon Yields, May 1998, Pg3
[44] JDW, Pakistan Needs up to 70 Nuclear Warheads, June 1998, Pg3
[45] JDW, India and Pakistan move to prevent nuclear disaster, March 1999, Pg16

military has played a larger role in governing the nation (and in initiating and supporting the bomb program) the decision is likely to be even more firmly lodged within an exclusive uniformed circle. The Defence Committee of the Pakistan Cabinet, chaired by the prime-minister, is believed to have taken the final deliberations to test the nuclear devices to respond to India.[47]

Nuclear Doctrine

To go to the effort to build and deploy any arsenal of weapons inexorably brings forth some sort of plan to use them. The more weapons a nation has, and the more types, the more involved and complex the planning becomes. In creating a war plan one starts with a target list. As nuclear war plans evolved in the United States and the Soviet Union there were two basic kinds of targets, "countervalue" and "counterforce".[48]

In the 1950s and 1960s the accuracy of the weapons-whether dropped by plane or delivered by missile was not very good, and thus cities became the "countervalue" targets of choice. As the weapons became more accurate and sophisticated, military, or "counterforce" targets took precedence. The goal of counterforce targeting is to destroy enemy nuclear forces before they can be fired (and destroy yours).[49]

However, targeting and deployments do not take place in a vacuum, and in the history of the Cold War, the ability to target enemy missiles precipitated its own crises and countermeasures. The temptation at least in the "theory" of deterrence to launch first was heightened. "Use-'em-or-lose-'em" was the popular description of this predicament. This might describe Pakistan's doctrine, given its military inferiority to India. After the nuclear tests, Pakistani Prime Minister Nawaz Sharif stated that "Pakistani nuclear weapons will deter aggression, whether nuclear or conventional", suggesting a first-use stance.[50]

Indeed, Pakistan's strategy is similar to the North Atlantic Treaty Organisations (NATO) stance in Europe during the Cold War. NATO realised that it could never match the Warsaw's Pact's conventional might. Therefore, it settled for doctrine that gave it the flexibility to use nuclear weapons first. Pakistan has adopted a similar strategy and hinted that it

---

[46] Ibid

[47] Ibid

[48] C.Philips, The Nuclear Casebook, Polygon Books, 1983, Pg16-17

[49] Ibid

[50] News International, Nuclear arms not to be used: Nawaz, June 1998, Pg1

could contemplate a nuclear first strike if its security were seriously threatened.[51]

Indian and Pakistani targets.

Nuclear targets may be broken down into three major categories: military targets; infrastructure, economic and industrial targets and cities. Military targets include military bases and headquarters, airfields, naval bases and specific nuclear weapons, concentrations of missiles or aircraft, both storage sites and operational units. Infrastructure and economic targets include energy facilities, nuclear reactors, dams, bridges, railroad hubs, factories and the like.[52]

Many military targets are close to major urban concentrations of which South Asia has no shortage. Bombay, Calcutta and Delhi have population of 12, 11 and 8 million respectively. Karachi, Lahore and Rawalpindi have population of 8, 5 and 2 million respectively. One bomb dropped on a large Indian or Pakistani city could cause millions of causalities.[53]

Delivery Vehicles

There has been further analysis and speculation about the nuclear capabilities and equipment of the two nations, including the development of a "triad" of nuclear capabilities by India. Only India has been explicit in its plans to develop a "strategic nuclear force". Pakistan has not stated whether it is set on deploying a dedicated nuclear arsenal, but undoubtedly India's actions will spur Pakistan along to reach India's technological level.[54]

The most likely method that India or Pakistan could use to reliably deliver a nuclear weapon today is by aircraft. Aircrafts were the initial method used by the first five nuclear nations. All initially carried gravity bombs. Later these planes were supplemented and/or replaced by many other types and also by various kinds of air-delivered cruise missiles and land- and –sea-based ballistic missiles.[55]

Nuclear-Capable Aircraft. India and Pakistan have several types of aircraft that would be capable of delivering nuclear weapons. India has a substantial number of fixed-wing aircraft that could be modified to deliver nuclear weapons. These include the Anglo-French Jaguar, the Mirage 2000 and the

---

[51] Ibid
[52] Sanat Biswas, Doomsday project, June 1994, Pg 84
[53] Ibid
[54] India Today, Future Fire, May 25, 1998, Pg23
[55] Albright & Zamora, op cit:26

Soviet-supplied MIG-27 and MIG-29 and the very sophisticated state-of-the-art Su-30MKI ultra long range strike aircraft (equivalent to the American F-15E).[56]

According to some sources, the Indian Defence Research and Development Organisation has perfected nuclear bombing techniques using the MIG-23 and MIG-27. For example, in the early 1980s, the Indian Air Force conducted fusing tests to verify that a nuclear bomb could be attached to and successfully released from its aircraft.[57] In 1997 Eric Arnett argued that India's acquisition of 315 Paveway II guidance kits to be used on 2000 Ib bombs as well as unknown number of similar smart weapons from Russia could with the help of its Air Force degrade the Pakistani nuclear strike potential compelling that nation into the "use of or lose it" (First Strike) dilemma and go in for an early or first use of its nuclear potential.[58]

Pakistan's military aircraft include nuclear-capable, U.S. supplied F-16 fighters, French-supplied Mirage 3/5 fighter-bombers and the co-developed Pakistani/Chinese JF-17 Thunder multi-role combat aircrafts. In the 1990 crisis with India over the uprising in Kashmir, Pakistani F-16s were reported to have been armed with nuclear bombs.[59]

<u>Indian and Pakistani missiles.</u> A ballistic missile has advantages and disadvantages: It is more likely to reach its intended target in the face of defensive measures. Each country has strategic reasons for pursuing this option: For India, a missile may be the only 'deterrent' possible against China; for Pakistan, which has a far smaller and less diverse air force than India, missiles may be the only reliable deterrent.[60]

India and Pakistan are developing and may deploy one or more types of ballistic missiles for nuclear weapon delivery. Since the tests, there has also been much speculation about India's sea-based missile capabilities.

<u>Nuclear Submarines.</u> India has been working since 1985 to develop an indigenously constructed nuclear-powered submarine, one that is based on the Soviet Charlie II-class design, detailed drawings of which are said to have been obtained from the Soviet Union in 1989.[61] Once the vessel is

---

56 Ibid

57 Sanat Biswas, Testing Time, 'Sunday Magazine', June 1998, Pg6

58 Arnett, Nuclear stability and arms sales to India, Arms Control Today, 1997, Pg3

59 India Today, India and Pakistan hours away from a nuclear war, 1994, Pg22

60 Jane Nolan, Ballistic Missiles in the Third World, Brookings Institutions, 1991, Pg89

61 JDW, Nuclear Submarine is being built in India, December 1994, Pg3

completed, around 2001-2005, it will be equipped with Sagarika cruise missiles and an advanced sonar system. The Sagarika began development in 1994 as a submarine-launched cruise missile (SLCM) which will have a range of at least 300 kms; it is projected for deployment around 2005.[62] By 2018, India has now developed and is in the process of testing much longer K-4 series SLBM and Agni series ICBMs.

North Korean Ballistic missile test[63] on March 7, 2017 shows the launch of four ballistic missiles by the Korean People's Army (KPA). This also shows have difficult it would be for a defending nation with a BMD capability to successfully shoot them all down. This is te kind of false narrative and a belief that a BMD capable nation holds resulting in an catastropic destruction of the countries involved.

---

[62] Ibid

[63] An Atomic-Weapons Expert's Worst-Case Scenario for What Trump Might Do With All That 'Access to the Nuclear Codes' - http://nymag.com/daily/intelligencer/2017/03/an-atomic-weapons-expert-on-the-worst-case-nuclear-scenario.html

CHAPTER 2: MISSILE RACE

An Emerging Ballistic Missile Race

One of the most dangerous missile competitions in the world today is the one between India and Pakistan, because they both have nuclear weapons and both have ballistic missiles to deliver them. These missiles could carry either conventional or nuclear weapons. Ballistic missiles are the weapon of choice for many developing nations. Their speed-to-target capabilities, invulnerability to defences, mobility, increasing accuracy and adaptability for carrying nuclear warheads all contribute to their inherently destabilising nature in regional rivalries. The relatively short distances between borders allow even tactical-range systems to have a significant impact upon regional balances.[64] The long-standing feud between the two countries has almost led to a nuclear face-off on at least occasion, in 1990.[65] We will look at the missile threat faced by both nations.

Indian Missile Forces

India has one of the world's most formidable missile programmes. India's military ballistic missile capabilities have become a lot more sophisticated in recent years. This has almost certainly become possible through India's space programme, which is one of the most advanced among the emerging

---

[64] Nolan op cit:88
[65] Ibid

missile powers.[66]

India started its ballistic missile development programme much earlier than Pakistan, aided in the development and deployment of missiles by both France and Russia. It has demonstrated the capability to launch satellites into orbit and has been a *de-facto* nuclear state since 1974. It has been almost universally accepted that India is well on the way to developing an intercontinental ballistic missiles (ICBM) with a range of greater than 12,000km.[67]

India's missile programmes are overseen by the Defence Research and Development Organisation (DRDO), which is in turn responsible for India's Integrated Guided Missile Development Programme (IGMDP). In 1983 the IGMDP programme saw the development and flight testing of five missile systems-the surface-to-surface (SSM) Prithvi and Agni missiles, surface-to-air (SAM) Akash and Trishul missiles and the anti-tank missile Nag. Using the experience gained from India's space programme, the IGMDP tested the Prithvi short-range missile in 1988. Though these designs are of concern for all countries in the region, for Pakistan the Prithvi and Agni missile programs have been followed with a greater degree of alarm. Of specific concern is the Prithvi missile, which has been labelled as 'Pakistan specific' by several Pakistani leaders. It is an SRBM with a range of 350km and a CEP (circular error probability) of 250m. It is capable of delivering a nuclear or conventional warhead of up to 1000kg.[68]

There are three variants of this missile: the SS-150, which is a battlefield support version for the Indian Army with a range of 150km and the ability to carry a payload of 1,000kg; the SS-250, which is a short-range missile (250km) with a warhead weight of 500-750 Kg for the Indian Air Force, (user trials are due to begin shortly); and the SS-350, which has a range of 350km and a warhead weight of 750-1,000 kg. Particularly alarming are reports that all versions of the Prithvi are nuclear-capable.[69]

In April, 1997, a minor crisis was sparked when news of Prithvi's deployment on the Pakistani border was leaked in the US press. India had moved its medium range missiles to prospective launch site at the Indo-Pakistan border near Jalandhar.[70] Meanwhile, repeated Indian announcements of induction of missiles (75 Prithvis being ordered by

---

[66] JDW, Asia's Missile Race Hots up, February 1994, Pg20
[67] Ibid
[68] Ibid
[69] JDW, India pressured to halt Prithvi productions, April 1995, Pg5
[70] Ibid

Indian Army and 25 by its airforce),[71] together with identification of missile sites, added up to a pattern of creeping deployment of the Prithvi. By 1996 an unspecified number of Prithvi missiles were believed to be in the possession of the Indian army's elite 333-missile group. This missile allows India to target Pakistan's capital city Islamabad and most of the close proximity defence establishments.[72]

Pakistan's reaction time to the pre-emptive launch of the missile is less than three minutes. Carried on mobile launchers and requiring little preparation time, the mobilisation of the Prithvi missile has marked a significant change in the strategic landscape.[73]

India has also tested its long-range, indigenously developed Agni missile. It is capable of carrying a nuclear payload, and has the potential to hit targets over 1500 kilometres away. The Indian government has also approved and advanced Agni system with a target range of 2500 kilometres, and is currently developing an ICBM called Surya with a range of over 12,000 kilometres.[74]

On the day of its nuclear tests, India test fired a home-made short range missile, the Trishul missile, at Chandipur. The Trishul, with a 50km range, has been developed for the Indian Navy. Russia is also assisting India in developing Sagarika, a 700km range sea-based cruise missile, also capable of a nuclear payload.[75]

Pakistan Missile Forces

Pakistan has escalated its own missile programme after the testing of Agni. However, unlike both Israel and India, Pakistan had no space launch programme at the time and therefore lacked the expertise to develop ballistic missiles. Because of the restraints imposed by Islamabad's limited scientific and industrial base, any Pakistani military missiles almost certainly had to be developed from foreign components with external technical assistance, or be obtained as a complete missile system package. However,

---

[71] Eric Arnett, Military Capacity and the Risk of War- China, India, Pakistan and Iran, Oxford University Press, 1997, Pg268
[72] JDW, Prithvi put back in production, 7 October, 1995, Pg17
[73] JDW, Asia's missiles race hots up, 1994, Pg20
[74] Ibid
[75] Ibid

Pakistan has consolidated its limited experience in this avenue, and has also used unconventional means to acquire the technology for its ballistic missile programme in order to counter an ascending Indian threat.[76]

Islamabad's attempts to indigenously develop ballistic missiles have been slow. Some uncertainty surrounds the exact designations of Islamabad's various missile systems due to its close co-operation with Beijing. Two missile systems were initially indigenously developed: the Hatf-1 and the Hatf-2, with ranges of 80 km and 300 km respectively. Despite their ability to carry a 500 kg payload, these missiles have a very poor circular error of probability (CEP).[77]

The failure to induct the indigenously developed Hatf I and II missiles has meant that the Pakistan government looked elsewhere for the technology to counter the Prithvi missiles. China has helped Pakistan, offering Pakistan the blueprint designs and manufacturing infrastructure required to build the M-11 ballistic missile. The production of the M-11 at Rawalpindi, which is capable of carrying a nuclear warhead to a range of 280 km, adds to the 30 M-11 missiles Islamabad received from China in 1992.[78]

Pakistan had developed the Ghauri missile, with a range of 1,500 km, in response to India's resumption of the Agni intermediate-range ballistic missile programme, putting New Delhi, Bombay and Madras within Ghauri's range. In the short-term, Pakistan's M-11 missile has a two-to-one range advantage over India's Prithvi I. (However, Pakistan's population centres are closer to the border than are India's which leaves Pakistan in a more vulnerable situation).[79] By 2018, Pakistan now produces a sophisticated range of ballistic missiles, such as the Shaheen 3 and the Ababeel MIRV missiles.

The latest purchase of the Russian SU-30 strike-aircraft, in addition to the existing squadrons of MIG-27s, Mirage-2000s and Jaguars have considerably enhanced Indian strike capabilities. According to Dr. Eric Arnett of the Stockholm International Peace Research Institute (SIPRI), the arms sales consisting of heavy laser-guided bombs and related equipment have been sold to the Indian Air Force over the past decade by Russia, Britain, America and Israel. These sophisticated arms have increased Pakistan's dependency on its range of ballistic missiles, such as the Ghauri missile etc., which is intended for deployment along the border with India.

---

[76] Ibid

[77] Ibid

[78] JDW, USA links Chinese ties to missile Exports, 1994, Pg6

[79] Ibid

"These weapons can destroy Pakistan's nuclear delivery systems even in hardened shelters. The Pakistan's Air Force's fear about the vulnerability of its aircraft must have been one of the main factors in the decision to develop and test the Ghauri ballistic missile".[80]

The development of ballistic missiles, with a delivery time of under three minutes, has raised the dilemma for both countries to use "use or lose" their nuclear weapons in an escalating crisis. Both nations might perceive the need for a 'first-strike' policy, to pre-empt the other side. There is an evident risk of lower-level officials in the field to seize the nuclear initiative without orders from the central government, due to the almost complete absence of command-and control centres at present. This instability is also exacerbated by the lack of early warning systems, or false-alarm contingencies, and also because speed of an attack would render any possible contingency ineffective.[81]

The disputed territory of Kashmir has the potential to trigger the next 'Cuban Missile Crisis'. Unknown to the Kennedy Administration in 1962, Soviet field commanders were authorised to launch nuclear missiles if the United States attacked Cuba. Given the absence of warning, the same is likely to be true of Indian and Pakistani military commanders in the vicinity of Kashmir. However, given the fact that India and Pakistan share common borders, the potential for a nuclear disaster appears much greater than any during the Cold War.[82]

Overall Nuclear delivery systems

A list of India's potential nuclear delivery vehicles is provided here. The nuclear weapons potential of India's estimated fissile material stocks will be equivalent to 150 warheads by the end of 2019.

---

[80] Eric Arnett, Delhi able to play nuclear trump in game for control of Kashmir, The Times, May 1998, Pg21
[81] Greenville, op cit:593
[82] Ibid

India, Possible Nuclear Delivery Vehicles, 2019

AIRCRAFT				
<u>Type-</u>	**Number Deployed**	**Range (Km)**	**Payload (Kg)**	<u>Speed</u>
Jaguar	117	2,600	4,750	Mach 1.5
Mig-27	65	1,100	4,000	Mach 1.7
Mig-29	63	1,500	3,000	Mach 2.35
Su-30MKI	250	3,000	8,000	Mach 2.0
Mirage 2000	50	1,850	6,300	Mach 2.2

Land-Based Missiles				
<u>Type-</u>	**Number Deployed**	**Range (Km)**	**Payload (Kg)**	<u>Classification</u>
Prithvi-150	Operational	150	1,000	BSRBM
Prithvi-250	Operational	250	500	SRBM

Prithvi-350	Operational	350	500	SRBM
Agni 1	Operational	700	1,000	MRBM
Agni 2/3/4	Tested/Dev	2,500-4,000	1,000	IRBM
Agni 5	Tested/Dev	5,000-8,000	Unknown	ICBM

Submarine-Launched Ballistic Missiles

Type-	Number Deployed	Range (Km)	Payload (Kg)	Classification
Sagarika	Tested/Dev	700-750	500	SLBM
Shaurya	Tested/Dev	3,000-3,500	500	SLBM

Source: federation of American scientists, Centre for Defence Information, PIADS intelligence Unit[83]

India's Nuclear capable aircraft

Jaguar	MIG-27 Flogger

---

[83] Centre for Defence Information (Internet)

MIG-29 Fulcrum

Su-30MKI Flanker

Mirage 2000

LCA Tejas

India's Nuclear Capable Missiles

Agni-5

Originated from: India
Possessed by: India
Class: Intercontinental Ballistic Missile (ICBM)
Basing: Road-mobile
Length: 17.5-20 m

Diameter: 2.0-2.2 m
Launch weight: 49,000-55,000 kg
Warhead: Unknown
Propulsion: Three-stage solid propellant
Range: 5,000-8,000 km
Status: Development
Tested: 2013

The Agni-5 is India's developing ICBM program, which consists of a three stage solid fueled missile potentially with MIRVed warheads. Though the missile has only been tested out to 5,000 km, classifying it as an intermediate range

Agni-4

Originated from: India
Possessed by: India
Class: Intermediate-Range Ballistic Missile (IRBM)
Length: 20.0 m
Launch weight: 17,000 kg
Payload: Single warhead, 800 kg
Warhead: Nuclear 20 or 45 kT, Fusion 200-300 kT
Propulsion: Two-stage solid propellant
Range: 3,500-4,000 km
Status: In development
In service: N/A

The Agni-4 is a two-stage solid propellant missile with a length of 20.0 m and a launch weight of 17,000 kg. Reports suggest that the Agni-4 can be fitted with a 20 or 45 kT nuclear warhead, or a 200-300 kT fusion warhead.

The Agni-4 is road mobile and carried by a truck TEL, unlike the Agni-3, which is primarily rail-mobile. The missile uses a combination of a ring laser gyro-based inertial navigation system and a redundant micro inertial navigation system for guidance, giving it double digit CEP.[84]

Agni-3

Originated from: India
Possessed by: India
Class: Intermediate-Range Ballistic Missile (IRBM)
csis.org/missile/agni-4/
Basing: Rail-mobile, possible road-based TEL
Length: 16.7 m

Diameter: 1.85 m
Launch weight: 48,000 kg
Payload: Single warhead, 2,000 kg
Warhead: Nuclear fusion 200-300 kT; possible MIRV version
Propulsion: 2-stage solid propellant
Range: 3,000-5,000 km
Status: Operational

The maximum payload of the Agni-3 is 2,000 kg. Some suggest a fusion warhead of about 200-300 kT will be the primary warhead and others claim the missile could carry MIRVs, conventional high explosives, or submunitions. The RV likely uses an imaging infrared or active radar terminal correlation seeker, reported to have an accuracy of 40 m CEP.

Rail-based launchers have exclusively fired the Agni-3 so far, though reports suggest future development of a truck TEL for a road-mobile version as well. In 2014, the Indian Ministry of Defense declared the Agni-3 part of the arsenal of the armed forces and the missile was part of its third user trial in April 2015.[85]

Agni-2

Originated from: India
Possessed by: India
Alternate name: Agni-II
Class: Medium Range Ballistic Missile
Basing: Road/rail-mobile
Length: 20.0 m
Diameter: 1.30 m
Launch weight: 16,000 kg
Payload: Single warhead, 1,000 kg
Warhead: Nuclear 150 kt or 200kt, HE
Propulsion: Two-stage solid propellant
Range: 2,000-3,500 km
Status: Operational
In service: 2004

The Agni-2 is a two-stage, medium-range, rail/road-mobile, solid propellant ballistic missile. In its present configuration, the missile is 20 m in length with a diameter of 1.3 m in the first and second stages. The missile

[85] Agni-3 - https://missilethreat.csis.org/missile/agni-3/

carries a warhead weighing up to 1,000 kg usually consisting of either 150 or 200 kT yield nuclear warheads, but also potentially high-explosive conventional versions. The Agni-2 uses a combination of inertial navigation and GPS in its guidance module as well as dual-frequency radar correlation for terminal guidance. Older Agni-2 models used four moving control fins in order to maneuver independently during the terminal phase. Newer models use side thrust motors instead. It has been reported to have an accuracy of 40 m CEP.[86]

Agni-1

Originated from: India
Possessed by: India
Class: Short-Range Ballistic Missile (SRBM)
Basing: Road/rail-mobile
Length: 14.80 m
Diameter: 1.30 m
Launch weight: 12,000 kg
Payload: Single warhead, 2,000 kg
Warhead: Nuclear 20 or 45 kT, HE, submunitions, FAE
Propulsion: Single-stage solid propellant
Range: 700-1,200 km
Status: Operational
In service: 2004

The Agni-1 is a short-range, road/rail-mobile, solid propellant ballistic missile. Falling between the short-range and medium-range categories, it fills the gap between India's Prithvi systems and the Agni-2.

The Agni-1 is 14.8 m long, 1.3 m in diameter, with a launch weight of 12,000 kg. It has a range of 700 km with an accuracy of 25 m CEP at a range of 860 km. At its maximum payload of 2,000 kg, the missile can carry a 20 or 45 kT nuclear warhead, or conventional explosives.[87]

---

[86] Agni-2 - https://missilethreat.csis.org/missile/agni-2/

[87] Agni-1 - https://missilethreat.csis.org/missile/agni-1/

Prithvi-I/II/III

Originated from: India
Possessed by: India
Alternate names: P-1, P-2, P-3
Class: Short-Range Ballistic Missile (SRBM)
Basing: Ground-launched
Status: Operational
In service: 1994

The Prithvi class of ballistic missiles make up most of India's arsenal of short-range ballistic missiles, useful for more tactical and battlefield uses. All of the missiles are road-mobile, allowing them to be deployed with maneuvering forces. The missiles have steadily improved their range from the 150 km Prithvi-I to the 350 km Prithvi-III and have progressed from liquid fueled to solid fueled over the same progression.[88]

---

[88] Prithvi-I/II/III - https://missilethreat.csis.org/missile/prithvi/

Dhanush

Originated from: India
Possessed by: India

Class: Short-Range Ballistic Missile (SRBM)
Basing: Ship-launched
Length: 8.53 m
Diameter: 1.0 m
Launch weight: 5600 kg
Payload: Single warhead, 500-1000 kg
Warhead: Nuclear, HE, submunitions, FAE, or chemical
Propulsion: Single-stage liquid propellant
Range: 250-400 km
Status: Operational
In service: 2010

The Dhanush missile is a short-range, ship-based ballistic missile – probably with a liquid propellant base – that is the naval version of India's Prithvi missile. The payload is presumed to be 500 to 1000 kg, with various warhead options including HE, submunitions, FAE, or chemical. It is powered by a single-stage liquid propellant and guided by an inertial system or GPS. The range is estimated in between 150 and 400 km, with an accuracy of 50 m CEP. Some sources suggest the accuracy is 25 m CEP.[89]

Sagarika / Shaurya

Originated from: India
Possessed by: India
Class: Short-Range Ballistic Missile (SRBM)/Medium-Range Ballistic Missile (MRBM)
Basing: sub-launched
Length: 10.8 m (Sagarika), 12 m (Shaurya)
Diameter: 0.8 m
Propulsion: Two-stage solid propellant
Range: 700-750 km (Sagarika), 3,000-3,500 km (Shaurya)

Sagarika

The Indian sub-launched ballistic missile (SLBM) program began in the 1990's. Work on an Indian SLBM likely began with the Sagarika or K-15/B-05 program, which has now given way to the K-4 or Shaurya program.

89 Dhanush - https://missilethreat.csis.org/missile/dhanush/

Sagarika

The Sagarika has a maximum range of 700 km and is powered by a two-stage solid propellant motor. It has a reported length of 10.8 m, a body diameter of 0.8 m, and a launch weight of 5,500 to 6,300 kg. The payload can be HE or nuclear with a weight of 500 to 800 kg. It uses Inertial Navigation System and Global Positioning System with terrain contour matching in the terminal phase.

Shaurya

Early testing of the Shaurya happened on land, with many suggesting that it was the land-based version of the Sagarika after tests in 2008 and 2011. The missile underwent its first undersea launch in March 2014 from a submerged barge, also demonstrating an expanded range of 3,000 km. The missile was tested again, firing at a depressed trajectory from an undersea barge and allegedly to a range of 3,500 km. The missile has already been tested from the Arihant. It is likely that the missile is intended to carry a nuclear payload to complete India's nuclear triad of delivery vehicles and could likely be outfitted with other conventional payloads.[90]

BrahMos

Originated from: Russia and India
Possessed by: Russia, India, Vietnam
Alternate names: PJ-10
Class: Supersonic Cruise Missile
Length: 8.0-8.2 m
Diameter: 0.67 m
Launch weight: 2,200-3,000 kg
Payload: 200-300 kg
Warhead: HE, submunitions
Propulsion: Liquid-fueled ramjet
Range: 300-500 km, 290 km export version
Basing: Ground-launched, Air-launched, Sub-launched, Ship-launched
Status: Operational

[90] Sagarika/Shaurya - https://missilethreat.csis.org/missile/sagarika-shaurya/

The BrahMos (PJ-10) is a short-range, ramjet powered, single warhead, supersonic anti-ship/land attack cruise missile developed and manufactured by India and Russia The BrahMos has a reported supersonic speed of between Mach 2.0-2.8, depending on the cruising altitude used. It has the stealth capability to evade radars and other detection methods, having greater strike power. It has an inertial navigation system (INS) for use against ship targets, and an INS/Global Positioning System for use against land targets. Terminal guidance is achieved through an active/passive radar.[91]

Prahaar

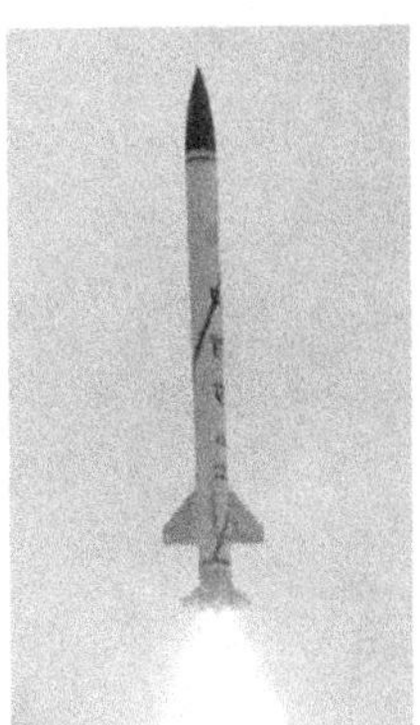

Originated from: India
Possessed by: India
Class: Short-Range Ballistic Missile (SRBM)
Basing: Road-mobile
Length: 7.3 m
Diameter: 0.42 m
Launch Weight: 1,280 kg
Payload: Single warhead, 200 kg
Warhead: Nuclear, HE, submunitions
Propulsion: Single-stage solid propellant
Range: 150 km

The Prahaar is a short-range, solid propellant, road-mobile ballistic missile designed for tactical strikes against close range targets.

The missile has a length of 7.3 m, a body diameter of 0.42 m, and a launch weight of 1,280 kg. It can carry a 200 kg payload with planned nuclear, HE, and submunition options. It can travel up to 150 km and is propelled by a single-stage solid propellant engine. The Prahaar is carried by the TATRA Transporter-Erector-Launcher vehicle and can hold six missiles per truck. Each missile is believed to be vertically launched, and they can be launched in salvo mode for multiple azimuth attacks.[92]

Nirbhay

Originated from: India
Possessed by: India
Class: Subsonic Cruise Missile
Length: 6.0 m
Diameter: 0.5 m
Launch weight: 1,500-1,6000 kg
Payload: 450 kg
Warhead: HE, submunitions, 12 kT nuclear potentially
Propulsion: Turbojet
Range: 800-1,000 km

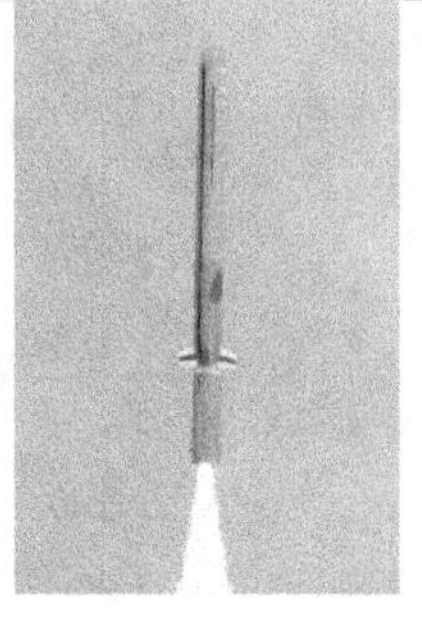

The missile uses a solid propellant booster motor that is jettisoned shortly after launch, switching over to a turbojet engine with a cruise speed of 0.65 Mach and a reported range of 800-1,000 km. The missile is guided by INS/GPS with an active-radar terminal seeker, and its accuracy could be improved both by the development of an indigenous Indian navigation satellite system and the potential of integrating the seeker from the BrahMos missile, which could be tested in December 2016.[93]

[91] BrahMos - https://missilethreat.csis.org/missile/brahmos/

[92] Prahaar - https://missilethreat.csis.org/missile/prahaar/

[93] Nirbhay - https://missilethreat.csis.org/missile/nirbhay/

A list of Pakistan's potential nuclear delivery vehicles is provided here. The nuclear weapons potential of Pakistan's estimated fissile material stock is 160 warheads by the end of 2019.

Pakistan, Possible Nuclear Delivery Vehicles, 2019

			AIRCRAFT	
<u>Type-</u>	Number Deployed	Range (Km)	Payload (Kg)	<u>Classification</u>
JF-17 Thunder	85	600	3,500	Mach 1.12
Mirage III/5	171	500	3,500	Mach 2.2
F-16	76	850	2,500	Mach 2

Land-Based Missiles				
Type-	**Number Deployed**	**Range (Km)**	**Payload (Kg)**	**Classification**
M-11	Storage (40-84)	280	800	SRBM
Hatf 9 Nasr	Operational	60-70	500	BSRBM
Hatf 1/A	Operational	70-100	500	BSRBM
Hatf 2 Abdali	Operational	180-200	500	SRBM
Hatf 3 Ghaznavi	Operational	290	500	SRBM
Shaheen 1/2	Operational	750-2,000	500	MRBM
	Operational	1,250-1,500	500-750	MRBM
Hatf 5 Ghauri	Tested/Dev	2,750	Unknown	MRBM
Shaheen 3	Tesyted/Dev	2,200	Unknown	IRBM
Ababeel	Operational	350-700	500	MRBM

Babur (GLCM)				
		Submarine Launched Cruise Missile (SLCM)		
Babur 3 (SLCM)	Tested/Dev	450-700	500	MRBM

Source: federation of American scientists, Centre for Defence Information, PIADS intelligence Unit[94]

CLASSIFICATIONS OF BALLISTIC MISSILES BY RANGE

BSRB	Battlefield	Short	Upto	Up to 94 miles
M	Range		150km	
SRBM	Short Range		150-699km	94-499 miles
MRB	Medium Range		700-	500-1,499
M			2,499km	miles
			2,500-	1,500-3,437
IRBM	Intermediate Range		5,499km	miles
ICBM	Intercontinental		+5,000km	+3,438 miles
SLBM Range	Submarine			No specific
	Launched			Classification

Pakistan's Nuclear capable aircraft

---

[94] Centre for Defence Information (Internet)

Mirage III/5

F-16 Fighting Falcon

JF-17 Thunder

JF-17 Thunder combat aircraft

Pakistan's most sophisticated type – the US F-16 Falcon Multi-role combat aircraft

Pakistan's Nuclear Capable Missiles[95]

---

[95] Missiles of Pakistan, Center for Strategic and International Studies (CSIS) -
https://missilethreat.csis.org/country/pakistan/?lcp_page0=1#lcp_instance_0

Ababeel (MIRV)

Originated from: Pakistan

Possessed by: Pakistan
Class: Medium-range ballistic missile
Basing: Road-mobile
Length: Unknown
Diameter: 1.7 m (est.)
Warhead: Nuclear, Conventional
Payload: Multiple Independently Targetable Re-Entry Vehicle
Propulsion: Solid-fuel
Range: 2,200 km
Status: In development
In Service: N/A

Tested: January 24, 2017

The Ababeel is Pakistan's first surface-to-surface medium range ballistic missile (MRBM), reportedly capable of carrying Multiple Independently Targetable Re-entry Vehicles (MIRVs). The Ababeel is a three-stage, solid-fuel medium-range ballistic missile with a reported maximum range of 2,200 km[96]

Shaheen 3 (MRBM)

Originated from: Pakistan
Possessed by: Pakistan
Class: Medium-Range Ballistic Missile (MRBM)
Basing: Road-mobile
Length: 19.3 m
Diameter: 1.4 m
Payload: Nuclear, conventional
Propulsion: Two-stage, Solid-propellant
Range: 2,750 km
Status: In development
Tested: March, December 2015
The Shaheen 3 missile is a two-stage, solid-fueled medium-range ballistic missile in development by Pakistan. The missile is reportedly capable of carrying both nuclear and conventional payloads to a range of 2,750 km, which would make it the longest range missile in Pakistan's strategic arsenal. It was first publicly displayed during a military parade in March 2016. The Shaheen 3 is road-mobile and reportedly mounted on a Chinese transporter erector launcher.[97]

Hatf 9 Nasr

Originated from: Pakistan

Possessed by: Pakistan
Alternate name: Nasr
Class: Short-Range Ballistic Missile (SRBM)
Basing: Road-mobile
Length: 6 m
Diameter: 0.4 m
Launch weight: 1,200 kg
Payload: Single warhead, 400 kg
Warhead: Nuclear, HE, submunitions

Propulsion: Single-stage solid propellant
Range: 60 km

---

[96] Ababeel MIRV - https://missilethreat.csis.org/missile/ababeel/

[97] Shaheen 3 - https://missilethreat.csis.org/missile/shaheen-3/

Status: In development
Tested: April 2011

The Hatf 9 Nasr is a Pakistani surface-to-surface short-range ballistic missile. The Hatf 9 is also believed to be a nuclear capable missile, but it could potentially carry an HE or submunitions payload as well.[98]

Hatf 8 Ra'ad

Originated from: Pakistan
Possessed by: Pakistan

Class: Subsonic Cruise Missile
Basing: Air-launched
Length: 4.85 m
Diameter: 0.5 m
Warhead: HE, nuclear, conventional
Propulsion: Turbojet
Range: 350 km

Status: Unknown

Tests of the Ra'ad have been largely conducted from Pakistan's Mirage III fighter jets, but there is potential for future systems such as the JF-17 fighter that could also host the Ra'ad. The Ra'ad has the given Pakistan a stand-off capability because it can deliver both nuclear and conventional payloads to a target from a 350 km range over and above the maximum range of the aircraft. Pakistani media reports the Ra'ad to be a "low-altitude, terrain hugging missile with high maneuverability" as well as "stealth capabilities [and] pinpoint accuracy."[99]

Hatf 7 Babur

Originated from: Pakistan
Possessed by: Pakistan
Class: Subsonic Cruise Missile
Basing: Ground launched
Length: 6.2 m
Diameter: 0.52 m
Launch weight: 1,500 kg
Payload: Single warhead, 450-500 kg,

reat.csis.org/missile/hatf-9/

[99] Hatf 8 Ra'ad - https://missilethreat.csis.org/missile/hatf-8/

nuclear capable
Warhead: 10-35 kT nuclear, HE, submunitions
Propulsion: Turbojet
Range: 350-700 km
Status: Operational
In service: 2010-present
Tested: August 2005

The Hatf 7 Babur is a short-range, turbojet-powered ground-launch cruise missile. The Hatf 7 is estimated to have a length of 6.2 m, a diameter of 0.52 m, and fold-out wings with a 2.5 m wingspan. With a launch weight around 1,500 kg, it is capable of carrying a 450 kg payload up to 700 km. The missile can be equipped with either a single 10 or 35 kT nuclear warhead, or up to 450 kg worth of conventional explosives (HE unitary or submunitions.[100]

Hatf 6 Shaheen 2

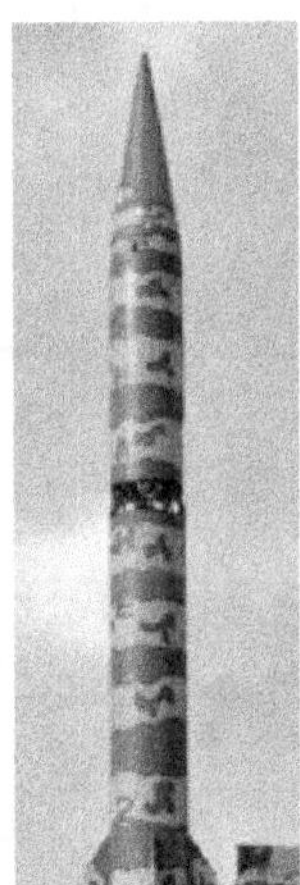

Originated from: Pakistan
Possessed by: Pakistan
Class: Medium-Range Ballistic Missile (MRBM)
Basing: Road-mobile
Length: 17.2 m
Diameter: 1.4 m
Launch weight: 23,600 kg
Payload: Single warhead, 700 kg
Warhead: 15-35 kT nuclear, HE, submunitions, chemical
Propulsion: Two-stage solid propellant
Range: 1,500-2,000 km
Status: Operational
In service: 2014-present
Tested: August 2005

The Shaheen 2 has a reported range of between 1,500-2,000 km. It is designed to carry a single warhead payload weighing 700 kg, though reports suggest that payloads up to 1,230 kg have been developed. Increasing the payload weight, however, may shorten the missile's range. The Hatf 6

---

[100] Hatf 7 Babur - https://missilethreat.csis.org/missile/hatf-7/

[101] Hatf 6 Shaheen 2 - https://missilethreat.csis.org/missile/hatf-6/

warhead can be equipped for a nuclear yield between 15 and 35 kT. There are also provisions to deploy the missile with conventional high explosives (HE), submunitions, fuel-air explosives (FAE), or chemical agents. It is launched from a transporter-erector-launcher (TEL). [101]

Hatf 5 Ghauri

Originated from: North Korea / Pakistan
Possessed by: Pakistan
Class: Medium-Range Ballistic Missile (MRBM)
Basing: Road-mobile
Length: 15.9 m
Diameter: 1.35 m
Launch weight: 15,850 kg
Payload: Single warhead, 700 kg +
Warhead: 12-35 kT nuclear, HE, submunitions, chemical
Propulsion: Single-stage liquid propellant
Range: 1,250-1,500 km
Status: Operational
In service: 2003

The Hatf 5 Ghauri is a medium-range, road-mobile, liquid-fueled ballistic missile deployed by Pakistan. It can carry a 700 kg warhead up to 1,500 km. Hatf 5's range and nuclear capability give it the ability to hold targets deep within Indian territory at risk , making it a core part of Pakistan's strategic missile forces.

Hatf 5A (Ghauri 2)

The Ghauri 2 is a medium-range, road-mobile, liquid propellant ballistic missile currently under development. It is a longer ranged variant of the Hatf 5, developed by replacing the heavier steel construction with an aluminum alloy and using improved propellants. It is expected to have a range of at least 1,800 km. [102]

Hatf 4 Shaheen 1

Originated from: China/Pakistan

Possessed by: Pakistan
Class: Short-Range Ballistic Missile (SRBM)
Basing: Road-mobile
Length: 12.0 m
Diameter: 1.0 m
Launch weight: 9,500 kg
Payload: Single warhead, 700 kg

Warhead: 35 kT nuclear, HE, submunitions, chemical
Propulsion: Single-stage solid propellant
Range: 750 km
Status: Operational
In service: 2003-present

The Hatf 4 Shaheen 1 is a short-range, road-mobile, solid-fueled ballistic missile. The Hatf 4 has a range of 750 km when carrying its standard payload and an accuracy of 200 m CEP. Its accuracy is provided by an inertial guidance system, and utilizes a "post separation attitude correction system" which helps increase its accuracy and may give it rudimentary ability to evade missile defense systems. It uses a single-stage, solid propellant engine and can carry a single high-explosive, chemical, or 35 kt nuclear warhead payload weighing up to 1,000 kg. The missile measures 12.0 m in length, 1.0 m in diameter, and has a launch weight of 9,500 kg.[103]

Hatf 3 Ghaznavi

Originated from: Pakistan

Possessed by: Pakistan
Class: Short-Range Ballistic Missile (SRBM)
Basing: Road-mobile
Length: 8.5 m
Diameter: 0.8 m
Launch weight: 4,650 kg
Payload: Single warhead, 700 kg
Warhead: HE, submunitions, 12-20 kT nuclear
Propulsion: Single-stage solid propellant
Range: 290 km
Status: Operational
In service: 2004

Hatf-3 appears to be an improved 'Scud' type ballistic missile. Its greatest military utility is in deployment against large, fixed

102 Hatf 5 Ghauri - https://missilethreat.csis.org/missile/hatf-5/

103 Hatf 4 Shaheen 1 - https://missilethreat.csis.org/missile/hatf-4/

targets such as military bases, airfields, and poses a threat to civilian urban areas. The Hatf 3 is around 8.5 m in length, 0.8 m in diameter, and 4,650 kg in launch weight. It can carry a single warhead up to 700 kg a maximum of 290 km.[104]

Hatf 2 Abdali

Originated from: Pakistan
Possessed by: Pakistan
Class: Short-Range Ballistic Missile (SRBM)
Basing: Road-mobile
Length: 6.5 m
Diameter: 0.56 m
Launch weight: 1,750 kg
Payload: Single warhead, 250-450 kg
Warhead: HE, submunitions, conventional
Propulsion: Single-stage solid propellant
Range: 180-200 km
Status: Operational
In service: 2005

The Hatf 2 Abdali is a short-range, road-mobile, solid propellant missile that entered service in 2005. Hatf 2 is equipped with an inertial guidance system and has a CEP of 150 m. It is estimated to carry a variable payload between 250 and 450 kg that affects its range, which falls between 180 and 200 km, and can carry a single high explosive or submunition warhead. It uses a single-stage solid propellant engine and has a length of 6.5 m and a width of 0.56 m.T he use of solid propellant and the TEL vehicle make the missile easy to store, transport and fire.[105]

Hatf 1 (Vengeance/Deadly missile)

Originated from: Pakistan
Possessed by: Pakistan
Class: Short-Range Ballistic Missile (SRBM)

Basing: Road-mobile
Length: 6.0 m
Diameter: 0.56 m
Launch weight: 1,500 kg
Payload: Single warhead, 500 kg
Warhead: Conventional
Propulsion: Solid propellant
Range: 70-100 km
Status: Operational
In service: 1992

The Hatf 1 is a short-range, road-mobile, solid-fueled ballistic missile. There are three versions: the 1, 1A, and 1B. The Hatf 1 is probably deployed with high explosive or chemical weapons, and although it could theoretically carry a tactical nuclear weapon, Pakistan has declared it to be non-nuclear. The missile is single staged, with a diameter of 0.56 m and is 6 m in length. Due to its solid propellant, it is simple to store, transport, and fire.[106]

---

[106] Hatf 1 - https://missilethreat.csis.org/missile/hatf-1/

Babur-3 Submarine-launched cruise missile (SLCM)

Originated from: Pakistan

Possessed by: Pakistan
Class: Subsonic Cruise Missile
Basing: Submarine-launched cruise missile (SLCM)
Length: 6.2 m
Diameter: 0.52 m
Launch weight: 1,500 kg
Payload: Single warhead, 450-500 kg, nuclear capable
Warhead: 10-35 kT nuclear, HE, submunitions
Propulsion: Turbojet
Range: 450-700 km[107]
Status: In development

In service: N/A
Tested: January 9, 2017

Babur 3 is a short-range, turbojet-powered Submarine-launched cruise missile (SLCM). According to ISPR's announcement, the Babur-3 missile, "is capable of delivering various types of payloads and will provide Pakistan with a Credible Second Strike Capability, augmenting deterrence."[108] Babur-3 is thought to have a range of 450 kilometers (some 280 miles) and some analysts have said it was 7oo km.[109] It is said that this SLCM will see Pakistan's nuclear deterrent head to sea—probably initially aboard its Agosta 90B and Agosta 70 submarines, but eventually, perhaps even on board new Type 041 *Yuan*-class submarines Pakistan is expected to procure from China.[110]

Harba Surface-to-Surface Anti-ship missile with Land Attack capability (ASCM/LACM)

Originated from: Pakistan

Possessed by: Pakistan
Class: Subsonic Cruise Missile
Basing: Surface-to-Surface Anti-ship missile with Land Attack capability (ASCM/LACM).
Length: 6.2 m
Diameter: 0.52 m
Launch weight: 1,500 kg
Payload: Single warhead, 450-

500 kg, nuclear capable
Warhead: 10-35 kT nuclear, HE, submunitions
Propulsion: Turbojet
Range: 450-700 km[111]
Status: In development
In service: N/A
Tested: January 9, 2017

Harba is a short-range, turbojet-powered Surface-to-Surface Anti-ship missile with Land Attack capability (ASCM/LACM). It is thought to be a 'Babur' cruise missile variant. According to the Pakistan Navy, the Harba Naval Cruise Missile is a surface-to-surface anti-ship missile with Land Attack capability. Harba is thought to have a range of 450-700 kilometers. It can also provide long range anti-ship and land attack capability and may add to Pakistan's nuclear deterrence (2nd Strike capability).[112]

Taimur Intercontinental Ballistic Missiles (ICBM)

Originated from: Pakistan
Possessed by: Pakistan
Class: Intercontinental Ballistic Missiles (ICBM)
Basing: Road-mobile
Length: Unknown
Diameter: Unknown

[107] South Asia's nuclear one-upmanship ramps up with Pakistan missile test - https://edition.cnn.com/2017/01/10/asia/pakistan-submarine-missile/index.html

[108] Safer at Sea? Pakistan's Sea Based Deterrent and Nuclear Weapons Security - https://twq.elliott.gwu.edu/sites/g/files/zaxdzs2121/f/downloads/40-3_ClaryPanda.pdf

[109] Pakistan Conducts 1st Successful Test of Submarine-Launched Cruise Missile - https://sputniknews.com/military/201701091049403419-pakistan-test-missile-sub/

[110] The Risks of Pakistan's Sea-Based Nuclear Weapons - https://thediplomat.com/2017/10/the-risks-of-pakistans-sea-based-nuclear-weapons/

[111] South Asia's nuclear one-upmanship ramps up with Pakistan missile test - https://edition.cnn.com/2017/01/10/asia/pakistan-submarine-missile/index.html

[112] Pakistan Test-fires Harba Anti-Ship Cruise Missile - https://quwa.org/2018/01/03/pakistan-test-fires-harba-anti-ship-cruise-missile/

Warhead: Nuclear, Conventional
Payload: Single warhead/Multiple Independently Targetable Re-Entry Vehicle
Propulsion: Solid-fuel
Range: 7,000+ km
Status: In development

Rumours[113] are stating that Pakistan is developing the Taimur missile[114], with a range of 7,000 km, is an ICBM under development. [115]

Tipu Sultan Intercontinental Ballistic Missiles (ICBM)

Originated from: Pakistan
Possessed by: Pakistan
Class: Intercontinental Ballistic Missiles (ICBM)
Basing: Road-mobile
Length: Unknown
Diameter: Unknown
Warhead: Nuclear, Conventional
Payload: Single warhead/Multiple Independently Targetable Re-Entry Vehicle

---

[113] Know more about Pakistan's most powerful missile Taimur - https://www.indiatvnews.com/news/world/know-more-about-pakistan-s-most-powerful-missile-taimur-14772.html

[114] Intercontinental Ballistic Missile OF Pakistan - http://f9view.com/intercontinental-ballistic-missile-of-pakistan

[115] Arms Control and Proliferation Profile: Pakistan - https://www.armscontrol.org/print/3201

[116] Deterence and Second Strike Capability of South Asia, Centre for Strategic and Contemporary Research (CSCR) - https://cscr.pk/explore/themes/defense-security/deterrence-second-strike-capability-south-asia/

[117] Tipu Sultan 15000 Km - https://www.facebook.com/permalink.php?id=1456469827937711&story_fbid=1458069467777747

[118] China helping Pak with ICBM: U.S. Congressman - http://www.thehindu.com/news/international/china-helping-pak-with-icbm-us-congressman/article8535575.ece

Propulsion: Solid-fuel
Range: 8,000 – 15000 km
Status: In development

Rumours[116] are stating that Pakistan is developing the Tipu Sultan missile, with a range of 7,000 - 15000 km[117], is an ICBM under development.[118]

Pakistani ballistic missiles

CHAPTER 3: NUCLEAR TRIAD

Nuclear TRIAD Complete - Babur-3 Submarine-launched cruise missile (SLCM)

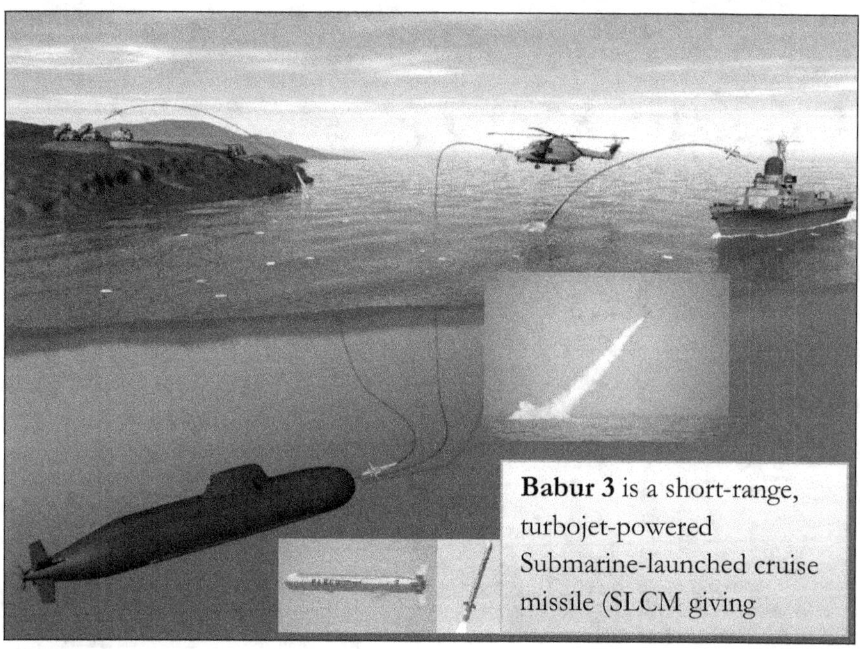

The Babur-3 cruise missile was fired from an underwater, mobile platform and hit its target with precise accuracy (thought to be Pakistan Navy's Agosta class submarines) in a test undertaken on the 9th of January 2017. The Babur-3 SLCM (submarine-launched cruise missile) with a range of 450 - 700 kilometers in land-attack mode is capable of delivering various types of payloads and will provide Pakistan with a credible second strike capability. This should enhance Pakistan's deterrence to any would be adversary.

The National Command Authority (NCA), is the organisation that oversees Pakistan's nuclear weapons. It is chaired by the Prime Minister of Pakistan (Chairman of this command) who oversee the employment, policy formulation, exercises, deployment, research and development, and operational command and control of nuclear weapons. The tri-service strategic commands all report to the Chairman in regards to development and deployment of nuclear weapons.

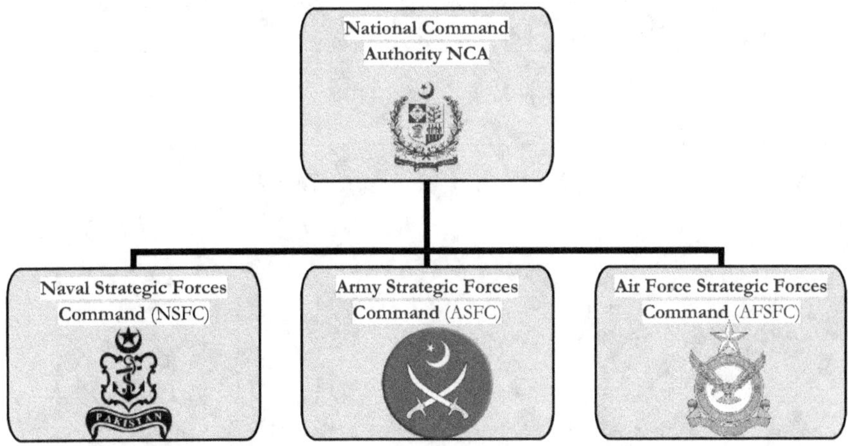

The Pakistan armed forces had set up Strategic Forces Command and had equipped the army and air force with nuclear weapons (delivery by missiles or aircraft). The Naval Stategic Forces command was lacking in this area, but with the advent of the Babur 3 SLCM this area has been given the capability. The successful testing of Babur-3 SLCM has given the Naval Strategic Force Command its nuclear-capable weapons.[119] This will complete Pakistan's quest for a TRIAD capability that will augment its deterrence capabilities. The second strike capability allows it to strike an adversary after receiveng a first strike from a hostile nation.[120]

---

[119] Pakistan fires nuclear-capable missile from submarine in the Indian Ocean (2017) Kerry B. Collison Asia News -
http://kerrycollison.blogspot.co.uk/2017/01/pakistan-fires-nuclear-capable-missile.html

[120] Pakistan completes nuclear triad, launches missile Babur-3 from submarine -
http://zeenews.india.com/asia/pakistan-completes-nuclear-triad-launches-missile-babur-3-from-submarine_1965794.html

Pakistani Shaheen 2 ballistic missile

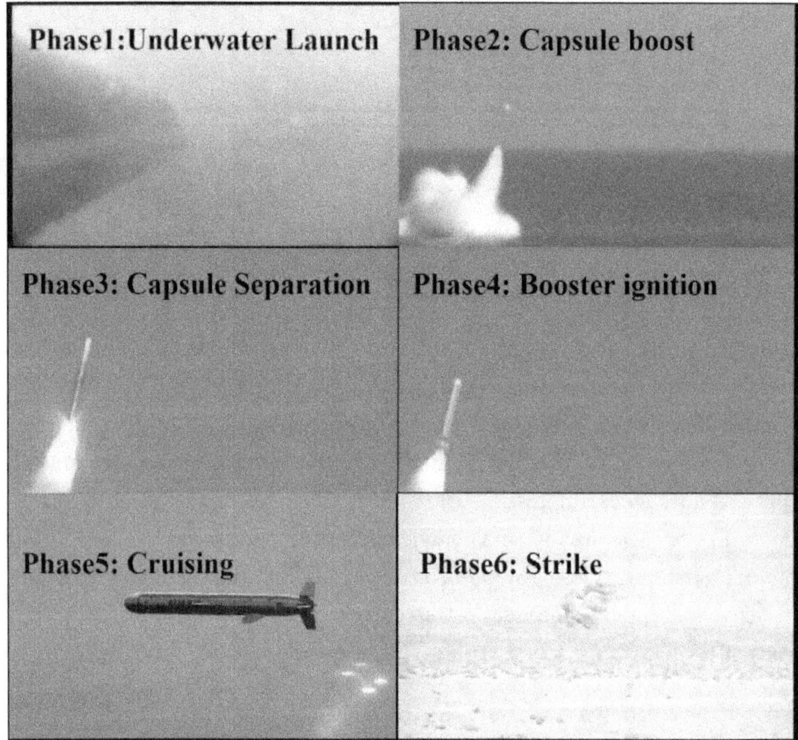

Pakistan on Thursday (29/03/2018) conducted another successful test fire

---

[121] Pakistan achieves 'credible second strike capability' with successful test of cruise missile Babur - https://www.thenews.com.pk/latest/298244-pakistan-successfully-test-fires-submarine-launched-cruise-missile-babur
https://defence.pk/pdf/threads/pakistan-navy-news-discussions.41/page-141

of indigenously developed Submarine Launched Cruise Missile Babur, having a range of 450 kms[121]

Pakistan Navy's Agosta Class submarine

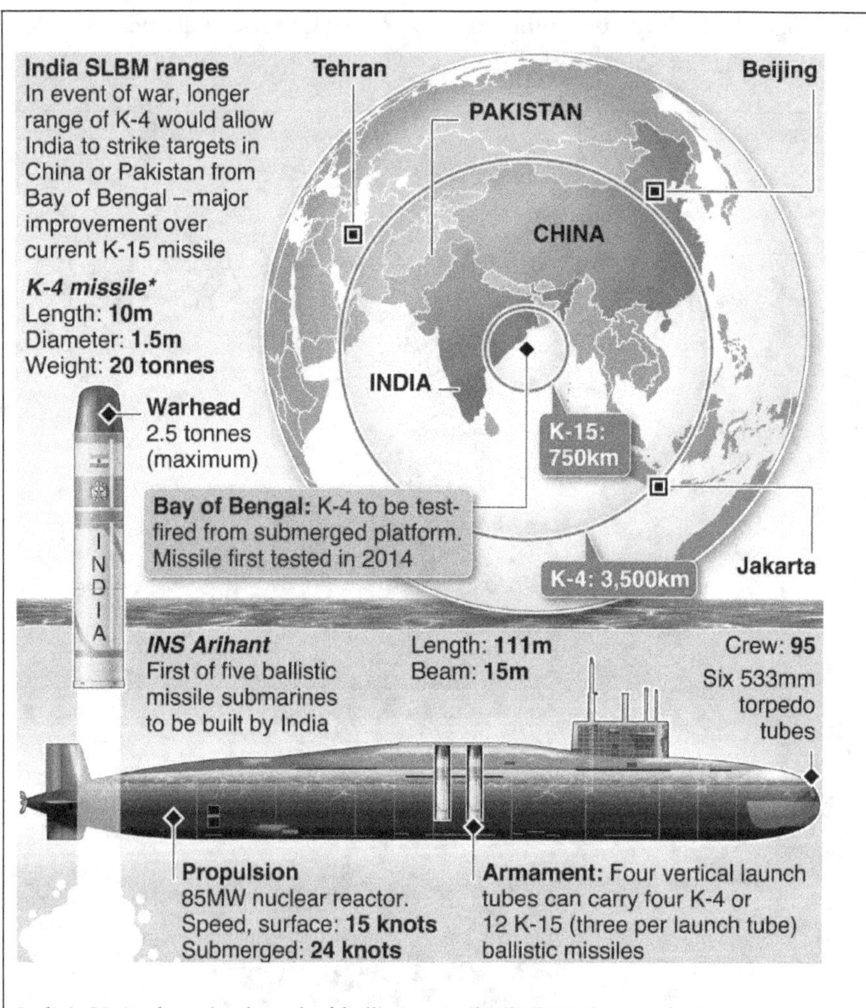

India's K-4 submarine launched ballistic missile (SLBM) from it Arihant nuclear submarine, gives it a nuclear strike capability against both China and Pakistan[122]

---

[122] Graphic news -
https://www.graphicnews.com/en/pages/35130/MILITARY-India-K-4-nuclear-missile?var=d

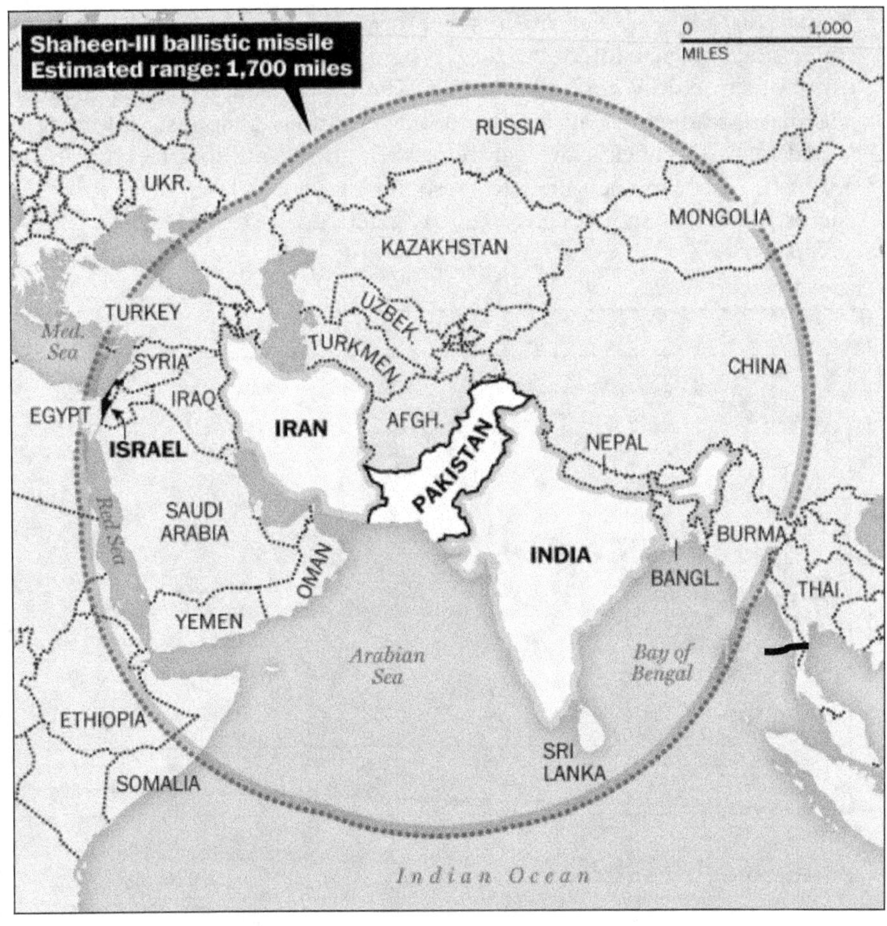

The Washington Post[123]

---

123 https://www.washingtonpost.com/

Both India and Pakistan are in the process of completing a TRIAD (three-sided military-force structure) system – in which nuclear weapons can be delivered by air, land and sea. The theory underlying the triad was that spreading the nuclear assets across various weapons platforms would make the nuclear arsenal more likely to survive an attack by an adversary and to be able to respond to a nuclear first strike successfully.This should give added deterrence to any would be adversary.

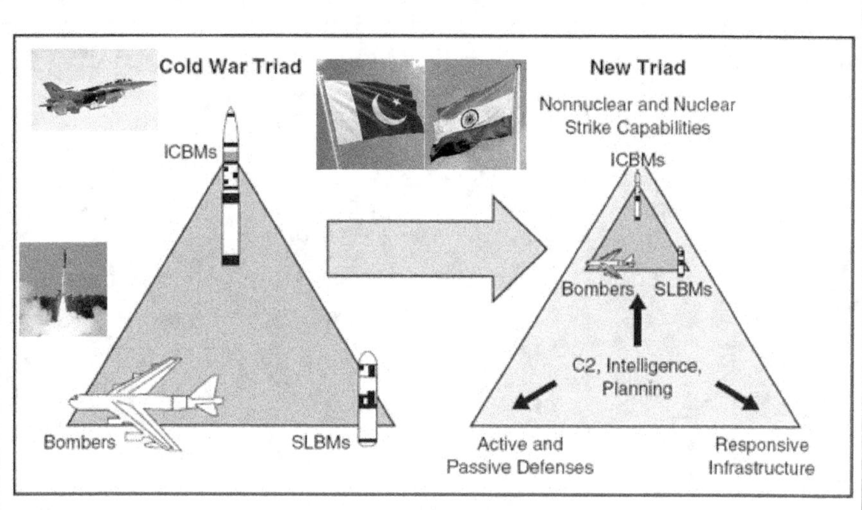

Pakistan, India in a naval and nuclear arms race - https://www.nextbigfuture.com/2015/10/700-nuclear-engineers-in-china-made.html

Pakistan's Nasr nuclear capable battlefield missile and french Rafael multirole combat aircraft (ordered by India)

CHAPTER 4: BALLISTIC MISSILE DEFENCE

Indian BMD will offer false sense of security

India has been working on a Ballistic missile Defence (BMD) shield to deter Pakistani missiles since 1999. In May 2001, the former US president George W. Bush prompted the Indian prime minister Atal Behari Vajpayee to acquire a BMD system – with assistance from the US and its allies (possibly to contain the missile threat from China and Russia). The US is seeing India as its counterweight to a rising China.[124]

Currently the Indian BMD has the capability of intercepting a missile in the terminal phase.

---

[124] Hasan Ehtisham, Indian BMD will offer false sense of security (2017) - https://tribune.com.pk/story/1503613/indian-bmd-will-offer-false-sense-security/

India has also joined the select group of nations that have a BMD system (US, Russia, Israel and China).[125] India has successfully test fired the indigenous interceptor missile Advanced Area Defence (AAD). Prime Minister Modi has said, **"with this India has demonstrated its ballistic missile defence capability".**

The BMD provides a two-layered shield – it provides protection both against ballistic missiles that are outside (exo) as well as inside (endo) the earth's atmosphere. The system India is developing is capable of intercepting and destroying incoming targets at an altitude of 15 to 25 kms.

The interceptor is a single stage solid rocket-propelled guided missile, equipped with sophisticated state-of-the-art technology. It is thought that the interceptor missile has its own mobile launcher, secure data link for interception, independent tracking and homing capabilities and sophisticated radars. On 11 February 2017, a test was conducted in which the interceptor destroyed an incoming Prithvi missile. The incoming hostile ballistic missile target was successfully intercepted at a high altitude (50 km). [126]

---

[125] India's impregnable ballistic missile defence interceptor shield is a strong message to Pakistan - http://www.financialexpress.com/india-news/indias-impregnable-ballistic-missile-defence-interceptor-shield-is-a-strong-message-to-pakistan/572233/

[126] India's impregnable ballistic missile defence interceptor shield is a strong message to Pakistan - http://www.financialexpress.com/india-news/indias-impregnable-ballistic-

Kings College University professor Harsh V. Pant states, **"The Indian BMD will fuel instability and affect bilateral relations between India and Pakistan, which might further lower the nuclear threshold and tempt Pakistan to go for a nuclear first strike".**[127]

According to the analysts Hasan Ehtisham, **"Indian BMD will offer false sense of security….. BMD capability will give India a false sense of security and will push India to go for a first nuclear strike. Thus, it could seriously undermine the deterrence stability in South Asia……The proficiency of the Indian BMD system is exceedingly debatable with respect to the geographical contiguity of India with Pakistan and China. During the Cold War, the distance between the US and the Soviet Union provided a necessary time for anti-ballistic missile (ABM) system to intercept an incoming missile. In case of India and Pakistan, the time gap is relatively too short to entirely attain necessary reconnaissance to efficiently intercept an incoming missile".**[128]

India's advance BMD missiles - Ashvin Advanced Defense (AAD) had successfully hit the incoming ballistic missile Dhanush, which was launched from Indian Navy vessel from the Bay of Bengal on the 15 May 2016 . It is argued that the primary reason for this test is to defend against any Pakistani ballistic missiles in the event of a conflict. It will also help India's Cold start doctrine of fighting a limited war with Pakistan under the shield of the BMD system.[129] India is also developing sophisticated technologies, such as nuclear submarines, SLBMs, Anti-satellite technologies (ASAT), cyber warfare technologies and shaping a Cold Start Doctrine (CSD) for a limited war. These technologies will impact on the stability and security of the regions deterrence.

According to the analyst Muhammad Suleman, **"The BMD system alone will severely undermine the strategic stability between these two**

---

missile-defence-interceptor-shield-is-a-strong-message-to-pakistan/572233/

[127] Ibid

[128] Hasan Ehtisham, Indian BMD will offer false sense of security (2017) - https://tribune.com.pk/story/1503613/indian-bmd-will-offer-false-sense-security/

[129]Muhammad Suleman, India's BMD System and Challenge to Strategic Stability - http://cpakgulf.org/2016/07/22/indias-bmd-system-and-challenge-to-strategic-stability/

relatively equivalent nuclear weapons states. It will not only disturb deterrence stability by limiting the enemy's capability to inflict 'unacceptable' damage, even if it can absorb a 'first strike', but it also instigates an opponent to strike first, if they believes they are threatened. Such developments increase the level of strategic instability so much that any false alarm, technical fault or miscalculation has the potential to become an accidental cause of war…..In times of crises, these technologies will cultivate a sense of military 'superiority 'in India, encouraging it to activate its provocative CSD strategy, under the cover of the ballistic missile shield and second strike capability".[130]

In view of the BMD and other sophisticated technologies that India is developing, Pakistan has begun to counter these measures by developing its own range of technologies to ensure that deterrence is maintained within the region. Pakistan. It has increased its ballistic missiles, nuclear weapons stockpiles, in the process of completing its TRIAD system (Aircraft, ballistic missiles, Submarine Launched Cruise Missiles). It has successfully tested the Ababeel multiple independently targetable reentry vehicles Vehicles (MIRVs) missile, has made improvement in tactical missiles and this has assured second strike capability. Pakistan has developed the Ababeel surface-to-surface medium-range ballistic missile, with a maximum range of 2,200 kilometres (1,400 miles). The missile was tested on 24 January 2017 and demonstrates the level of Pakistan's sophistication in addressing its security needs. The missile has the ability to carry either conventional or nuclear warheads, and is claimed to use multiple independently targetable re-entry vehicles (MIRV). This would enable the Ababeel MIRVed missile to overwhelm any BDM defences that India could put up, thus enhancing its second strike capability and deterrence.[131]

---

[130] Ibid

[131] Muhammad Suleman, India's BMD System and Challenge to Strategic Stability - http://cpakgulf.org/2016/07/22/indias-bmd-system-and-challenge-to-strategic-stability/

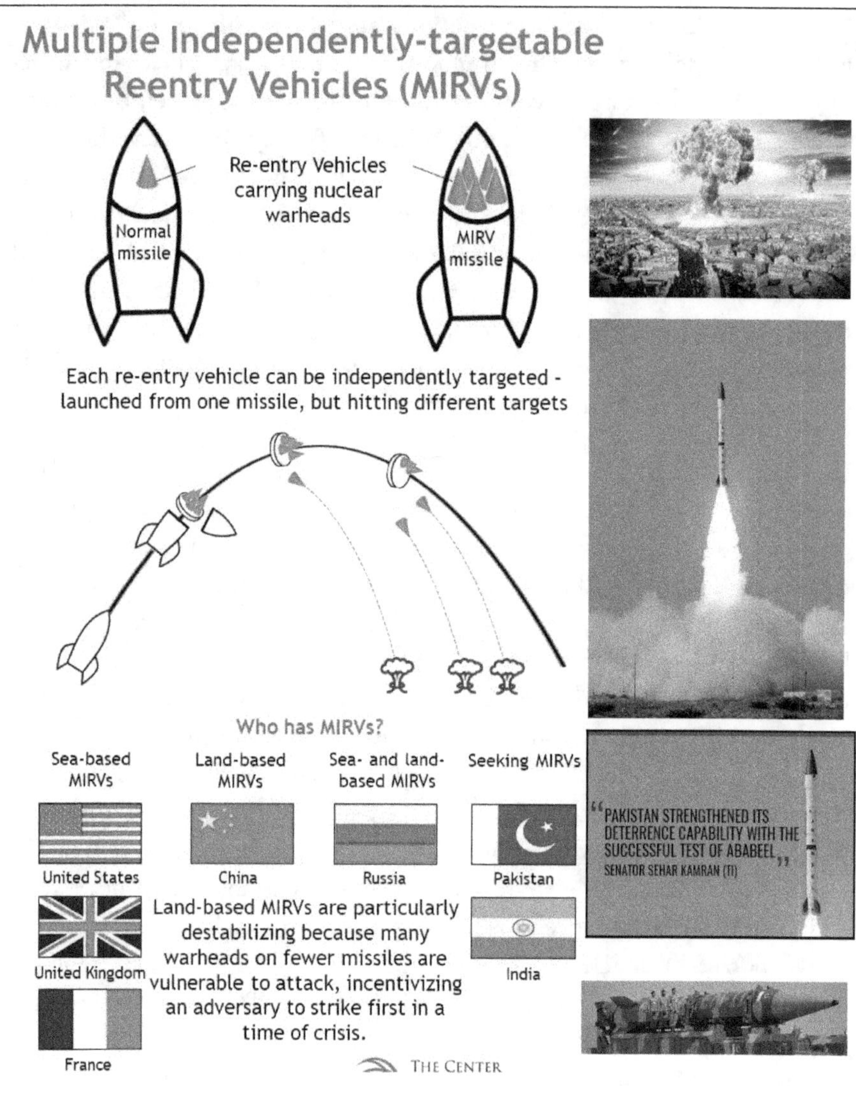

Currently 5 countries have known MIRV capability with Pakistan test's of the Ababeel missile making it the sixth nation in the world to possess this capability. It is thought that India will also follow and suit and develop its own MIRV capability. The use of MIRVs on submarines is considered less

---

[132] Multiple Independently-targetable Reentry Vehicle (MIRV) - https://armscontrolcenter.org/multiple-independently-targetable-reentry-vehicle-mirv/

destabilizing than on land-based missiles because the difficulty of finding nuclear submarines makes strikes against them unlikely. In January 2017 Pakistan tested a MIRVed missile (Ababeel). Senior Indian defense officials have indicated that India's Agni-class of missiles will eventually have MIRVed capability.issiles will be MIRVed.[132]

Image/pixabay.com/Patriot missile defence

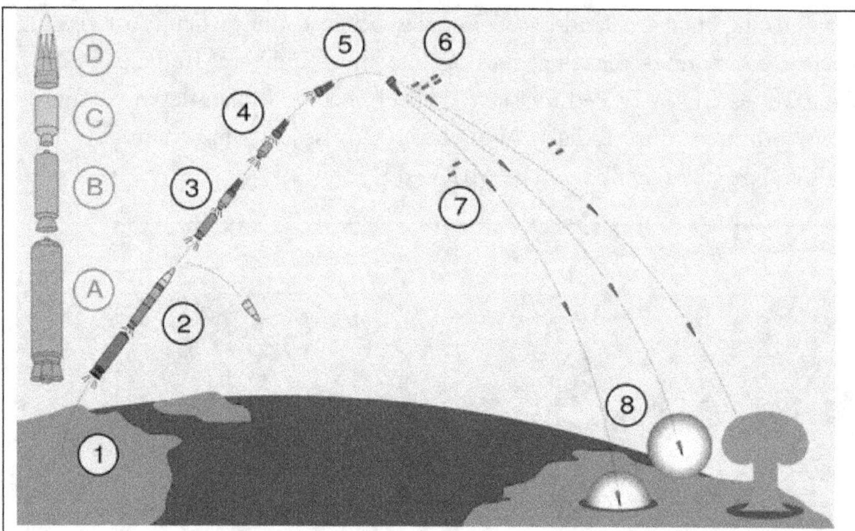

The above diagram showing the different stages of a MIRVed ICBM – in this case the US Minuteman III ballistic Missile.[133] The following sequences are given:

1. The missile launches out of its silo by firing its 1st stage boost motor (A).
2. About 60 seconds after launch, the 1st stage drops off and the 2nd stage motor (B) ignites. The missile shroud is ejected.
3. About 120 seconds after launch, the 3rd stage motor (C) ignites and separates from the 2nd stage.
4. About 180 seconds after launch, 3rd stage thrust terminates and the Post-Boost Vehicle (D) separates from the rocket.
5. The Post-Boost Vehicle maneuvers itself and prepares for re-entry vehicle (RV) deployment.
6. The RVs, as well as decoys and chaff, are deployed during backaway.
7. The RVs and chaff re-enter the atmosphere at high speeds and are armed in flight.
8. The nuclear warheads detonate, either as air bursts or ground bursts.

The significance of MIRV missile for Pakistan is that it becomes a force multiplier by delivering many warheads via one missile. It gives Pakistan the ability to strike multiple targets with a high level of precision and will

---

[133] ICBM diagram -
https://en.wikipedia.org/wiki/Wikipedia:Featured_picture_candidates/ICBM_diagram

disrupt or destroy the defensive capabilities of its adversary (radars and other sophisticated defence technolgies that woul aid an adversarys BMD capability). As technologies emerge further in the subcontinent, the costly arms race could lead to a nuclear nightmare if confidence building measures are not introduced by India and Pakistan. In conjuction with other nuclear powers, a serious attempt in reducing weapons of mass destruction and related technologies should be implemented to make the world a safer place for its inhabitants.[134]

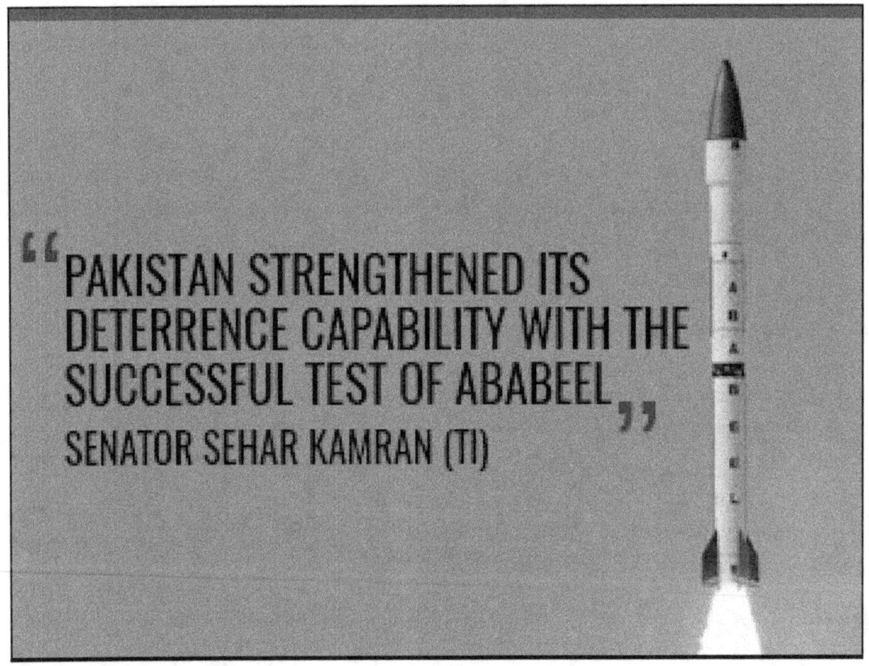

---

[134] Pakistan's Ababeel ballistic missile ensures strategic stability in South Asia - https://www.globalvillagespace.com/pakistans-progression-in-ballistic-missiles-will-it-neutralize-india-or-bring-another-wave-of-arm-race/

CHAPTER 5: RISK OF INADVERTENT WAR

Risk of inadvertent war?

Undermining the apparent 'stability' that conventional and nuclear forces have given to the region is their shared common border, and the ongoing dispute over Kashmir, which both sides lay claim to. The introduction of ballistic missiles has only exacerbated this insecurity. Add to this the psychological ingredient of nuclear superiority, and the likelihood of incoherent decision-making increases. The shared border leaves a very small margin for error at the outset of any hostilities compared to that of the superpowers, thus increasing the risk of conflict through miscalculation and misconception.[135]

During the early years of the Cold War, when nuclear weapons could only be delivered by aircraft, both superpowers had many hours to determine whether an alert was a false alarm. The advent of ICBMs reduced this to 25 minutes, then 10 minutes with submarine-launched ballistic missiles (SLBMs). India and Pakistan's close borders produce an almost negligible warning time of three minutes, reducing the chances of defining a false alarm from a real attack.[136]

Anti-tactical ballistic missiles (ATBMs)

Compounding Pakistan's concern were credible reports of India's pursuit of an anti-tactical ballistic missile (ATBM) capability, either through indigenous design or purchasing off-the-shelf, in the early 1990s. This was through the development of an improved version of the Akash system, with India also on the lookout for a more advanced system. It has also asked Israel for designs of its Arrow ATBM, whilst negotiating with Russia for its S-300V missile systems (touted as similar to the U.S. Patriot system). The acquisition of an advanced air defence system with ATBM capability will give India the capability to intercept tactical ballistic missiles with ranges of over 300km. India claims to want these systems for the defence of New Delhi and Bombay.[137]

---

[135] Zian Mian, No time to think, Jang Publishers Ltd, 1998, Pg10
[136] Ibid
[137] Afzal Mahmood, Mini-Starwars in Asia? Dawn Publishers Ltd, 1999, Pg1

India's interest in missile defences appears to be driven primarily by Pakistan's acquisition and development of M-11 and Hatf series of ballistic missiles in the early 1990s. Pakistani defence officials have acknowledged that Pakistan would find such as development threatening and could respond by increasing its nuclear and missile capabilities.

Strategic Implications of an Indian Missile Defence System

A sophisticated Indian air defence system with ATBM capabilities could seriously undermine Pakistan's reliance on the M-11/Ghauri ballistic missile and on its tactical strike aircraft (e.g, F-16, JF-17 and reconditioned Mirage III) as its primary nuclear- capable delivery systems. India has also modernised its air defences with the purchase and license production of Russian-made Su-30MKI fighter-bombers and the Tunguska low-altitude air defence system.[138]

Moreover, its planned acquisition of French Mirage 2000 fighters has been held up by financial and political problems. Pakistan's missile programmes are driven by a desire to augment limited offensive air capabilities against India (which holds a nearly 2:1 advantage in combat aircraft) and to field a more effective delivery system. Therefore, without a credible aerial delivery capability, Pakistan will have to rely mainly on ballistic missiles to overwhelm India's defences. Unable to match India's defensive systems, Pakistan's initial response could entail increasing the number of nuclear weapons and delivery systems available at short notice, in order to restore its deterrent.[139]

India's acquisition of an ATBM could therefore destabilise the existing nuclear balance by depriving Pakistan of an assured strike capability, thus allowing India to engage in a conventional war, or invade Pakistan-held Kashmir, without fear of nuclear retaliation. Given the large imbalance of conventional forces between India and Pakistan, the outcome of such a conflict is not in doubt. The danger lies in a sharp reaction to any perceived 'ill-intended' exercise, such as the 'brass-tack' military exercise by India in 1987, which heightened tensions between the two countries.[140]

Pakistan's options would be either to match India's defences, or overwhelm India's capability. Its short-term prospects for either are slim, due in part to its own economic conditions and also to the punitive sanctions imposed on both states by the West after the 1998 nuclear tests. The United States is

---

[138] Ibid

[139] Ibid

[140] Ibid

currently barred from supplying Pakistan with any military equipment due to the Pressler Amendment, and Russia's close relations with India make major arms sales to Pakistan unlikely. Pakistan's long-term prospects of acquiring a missile defence system are greater through China, which has renewed its close relationship with Pakistan after India's nuclear tests. China is believed to be working on its own ATBM capability.[141]

Pakistan- notwithstanding its smaller defence budget and resources base-is capable of building up its nuclear offensive deterrent incrementally. This could entail increasing the number of nuclear weapons available for both missile and aircraft delivery, acquiring cruise missiles, and developing decoys and penetration aids to saturate India's active defences. The introduction of an ostensibly defensive ATBM capability into by India has increased the potential of a full-fledged, South Asian nuclear arms race.[142]

Pakistan's Shaheen-III medium-range ballistic missile (MRBM) is carried by a 16-wheel transporter erector launcher (TEL)

---

[141] Mahmood, op cit:3
[142] Ibid

An Indian Agni-II intermediate range ballistic missile on a road-mobile launcher, displayed at the Republic Day Parade on New Delhi's Rajpath, January 26, 2004.[143]

143

https://en.wikipedia.org/wiki/India_and_weapons_of_mass_destruction#/media/File:Agni-II_missile_(Republic_Day_Parade_2004).jpeg

CHAPTER 6: KASHMIR SCENARIO – POTENTIAL FOR A NUCLEAR WAR

India and Pakistan have to resolve the Kashmir issue amicably in order to avoid a never ending cycle of conflict. This conflict is having an adverse effect on the economies and the welfare of the people of South Asia.

Kashmir Scenario – Potential for a nuclear war

Kashmiri protestors in
Indian occupied Kashmir

Militants/freedom fighters
in hot pursuit from Indian
troops cross the border into
Pakistan.

3

Border Skirmish between
Pakistan and India – due to hot
pursuit of the
militants/freedom fighters.
Clashes occur.

4

Indian border patrols

Pakistani border patrols

Pakistan anti-tank/anti-bunker missile

Kashmir's Young Rebels

Indian soldiers

Limited border conflict escalates to a major full blown conflict

4th major Indo-Pakistan war starts. Indian numerical supremacy takes toll on Pakistani forces.

Indian Artillery

Pakistani firepower

Pakistani Multiple Rocket
Launchers

Indian MBT and Artillery

Indian Air Force Strike aircraft

7

Pakistan begins to lose
significant forces and
territory – India is
threatening to cross
Pakistan's 'Red' line.
Pakistan contemplates in

8

India reacts with firing Nuclear
ballistic missile – nuclear
conflict erupts. India aims to
destroy all known
nuclear/launch sites in
Pakistan. First major strike –

the use of nuclear weapons on Indian troop formations, as a warning. It fires tactical nuclear weapons on Indian military formations – via Nasr battlefield nuclear missile. Watching an Indian response, Pakistan ready to fire its main long-range nuclear capable ballistic missiles.

with the plan to destroy all nuclear capability of Pakistani forces.

Indian Prithvi Nuclear ballistic Missile

Indian Agni nuclear capable ballistic missile

Tactical nuclear weapons

Pakistan counter-attacks (second strike capability from its submarines) with SLCM or SLBM in an attempt to destroy Indian forces/cities.
9
Indian second strike capability has been initiated from its submarines – aim to destroy remaining Pakistani forces.
10
INS ARIDHAMAN SSBN
India's Next Generation Nuclear Submarine
Babur 3 SLCM (Nuclear) – Second strike capability

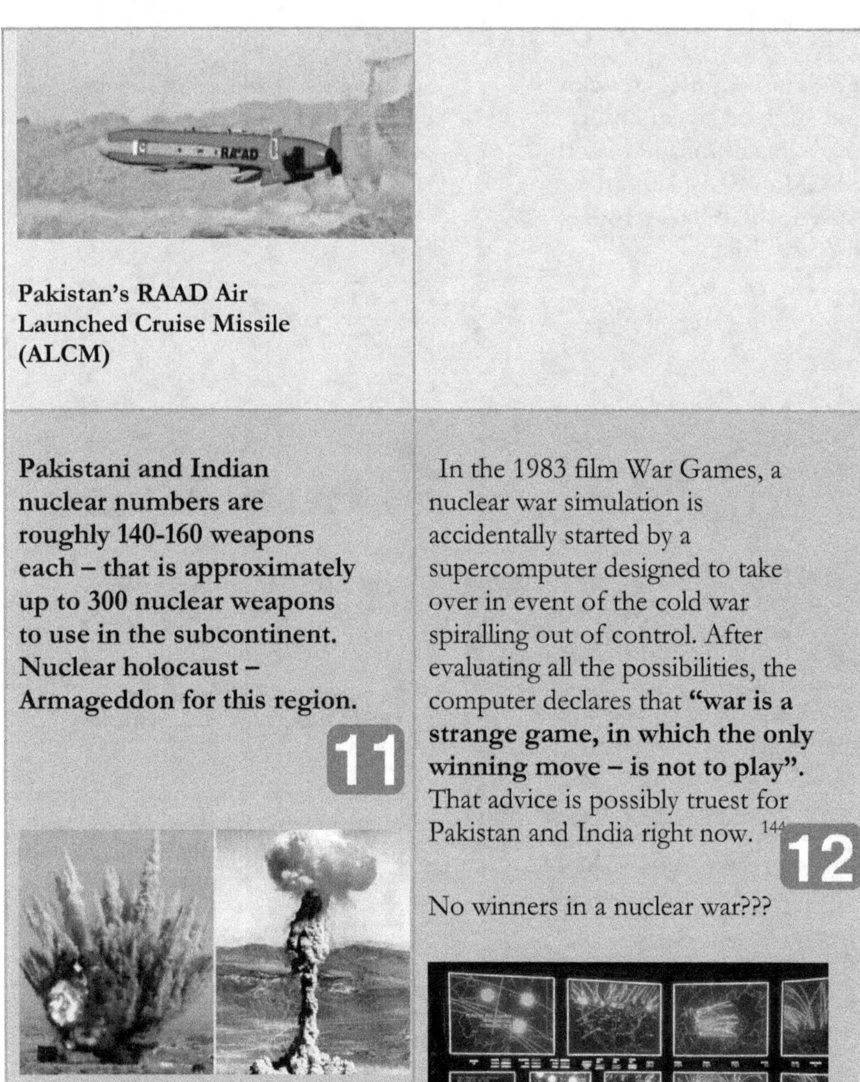

Pakistan's RAAD Air Launched Cruise Missile (ALCM)

Pakistani and Indian nuclear numbers are roughly 140-160 weapons each – that is approximately up to 300 nuclear weapons to use in the subcontinent. Nuclear holocaust – Armageddon for this region.

In the 1983 film War Games, a nuclear war simulation is accidentally started by a supercomputer designed to take over in event of the cold war spiralling out of control. After evaluating all the possibilities, the computer declares that **"war is a strange game, in which the only winning move – is not to play".** That advice is possibly truest for Pakistan and India right now. [144]

No winners in a nuclear war???

---

[144] Raghu Raman, Why war with Pakistan—is not an option -
https://medium.com/@captraman/why-war-with-pakistan-is-not-an-option-3ccfa25a1529

The unthinkable nuclear nightmare! 12

CHAPTER 7: ARMS CONTROL AND CONFIDENCE-BUILDING MEASURES

Arms Control and Confidence-Building Measures

The nuclear tests in 1998 have established a form of defence equilibrium. The consequences of a nuclear conflict would be enormously destructive, with neither side being a winner. There is a real concern that the long-standing hostility between India and Pakistan could overwhelm any deterrent advantage gained from these weapons. The need for continued, relentless dialogue is all too apparent given the short history of both nations.

Over the years Pakistan has proposed numerous bilateral nuclear arms control initiatives with India, declaring, for example, that it would be prepared to join the NPT or accept other non-proliferation measures if India did so. India has rejected these proposals, arguing that they do not address the nuclear threat India faces from China and that nuclear disarmament questions should be addressed as a global, rather than as a regional issue. Pakistan and India have, however adopted a number of bilateral confidence-building measures, including a military-to-military hot-line and an agreement, which entered into force in January 1991, prohibiting the two states from attacking each other's nuclear installations. Lists of facilities covered by this agreement are now also exchanged periodically.[145]

Actual measures Pakistan and India could take

Tackle the Kashmir Problem Positively.

It is obvious that nuclear risk reduction will not get anywhere if there is no movement towards a broader settlement on Kashmir. Pending a solution to the dispute, progress is essential in dealing with the immediate sources of tension to build a climate of normalcy and pave the way to a just Kashmir settlement.

The two nations should attempt to humanise the problem of Kashmir, rather than engage in political and military tit-for-tat. The alleviation of human suffering in Kashmir should be the overriding concern of both sides. Confidence building measures could include the safeguarding of fundamental human rights, unconditional release of Kashmiri prisoners, unifying divided families, providing access to international humanitarian organisations in occupied Kashmir and granting Kashmiri's the right to a fair trial. This is by no means an exhaustive list, but illustrative of how to humanise the problem in order to deal with its most urgent dimensions.[146]

Limitations placed on missile deployments and warheads.

Limitations on offensive weapon systems, curtailment of forward build-up of military cantonments and airfields would be a positive gesture for peace. None of these measures would deprive India or Pakistan of deterrence or defence capability. While Pakistan has around 8 or so forward airfields, India has over 15 forward and 16 medium-range airfields. Apart from these, it has only 9-10 remaining military fields in the rear. Given the range of India's military aircraft and its Prithvi missiles, closing some of these forward airfields would restore confidence on both sides.[147] Secondly, an overt nuclear deterrence will now allow Pakistan to cut down on conventional defence spending – this is of vital interest to Pakistan. A beginning can be made on a treaty similar to the Conventional Forces in Europe Treaty. The logic of that treaty is equally applicable here, i.e. to reduce the chances of surprise attacks and stabilise the military balance, rather than eliminating military forces per se from the region.[148]

---

[145] Ashok Kapur, Pakistan's attitude to the NPT, Parchment Press, 1993, Pg25
[146] Maleeha Lodhi, Nuclear Risk reduction and Conflict-Resolution in South Asia, Jang Publications Ltd, 1998, Pg11
[147] Ibid
[148] Ibid

Reduce the number of Soldiers and their main equipment deployed along the borders.

Both sides should focus on limitations on the number of troops, armoured and mechanised formations from each other's borders, eventually leading to the reduction of conventional offensive capabilities. India's rationale of the threats from other neighbours like China or even Bangladesh does not hold within this context, since the armoured and mechanised formations are really only suitable, terrain-wise, against Pakistan. Also a mutual agreement not to deploy armoured divisions in areas where surprise attack is possible, specifically in the central and desert plateau along the Indo-Pakistan border. That whole area can be declared a tank-free zone.

A reduction in new weapon systems.

A move towards prohibiting the induction of the latest technologies and weapons into their conventional forces would also be welcome. The underlying mutual minimal nuclear deterrence would lessen the need for the importance of 'state-of-the-art' weapons technologies. Defence acquisitions of new weapon systems and new technology should be made the subject of mutual discussions. For this reason, any nuclear risk reduction objective requires addressing the conventional asymmetry between Pakistan and India to reduce Pakistan's greater need for missiles. These are already regarded as both feasible and cost-effective by its defence planners.

Increase nuclear co-operation between each other.

The eventual recognition and acceptance of each other's nuclear weapons capability can lead to co-operation, if desired, especially in terms of multilateral nuclear fuel centres, where technology can be jointly controlled. Given the problem both countries face in terms of conventional power generation, including the costs, nuclear power can become a viable alternative. Here the security route can eventually lead to direct economic benefits.[149]

India and Pakistan should sign a Non-Aggression Pact.

Pakistan must move towards evolving a non-aggression pact – either at the bilateral level or the South Asian nations multilateral level. Such a pact differs from a no-war pact and does not deny the use of the military option in self-defence – it only denies parties the option of aggressing against other parties to the pact. It calls on both sides to commit to agreements not to

---

[149] Ibid

aggress against each other within a military framework. This implies that both India and Pakistan cannot simply intensify exchanges along the line of control (LoC) into an all-our war against their international borders. A non-aggression pact will further build on the confidence-and security-building measures (CSBMs) involving the hot-line, communication facilities between commanders on both sides of the LoC and other such measures – some of which are already in place but not adhered to strictly.[150]

Sign the major International Treaties.

Along with a proposal for a non-aggression pact, Pakistan must go a step further in its moves towards joining the mainstream nuclear powers by agreeing to sign the **CTBT** as a nuclear weapon state. Already Pakistan has made one wise move in this field by declaring its intentions of not exporting its nuclear technology.

The Comprehensive Test Ban Treaty (CTBT) - Pakistan has sensibly delinked the issue of its signing the CTBT from what India does. The reason for this is simple – neither India nor Pakistan can conduct anymore nuclear tests underground – at least in the foreseeable future. So there is no need for Pakistan to hold out on the CTBT. As for the CTBT itself, it deals specifically with nuclear tests which it seeks to prohibit completely. Its verification and on – site clauses also deal with test sites and not with reactors and other weapons – producing installations.[151]

The Non-Proliferation Treaty (NPT) - Pakistan has been under considerable pressure for a number of years to unconditionally sign the NPT. India carried out nuclear tests in 1974 and has not signed the NPT. Pakistan has insisted that it will not sign the treaty until India has also done so.[152]

Missile Technology Control Regime (MTCR) - With the successful testing of the Ghauri and Agni missiles, Pakistan and India can both become party to the MTCR. This would allay fears that Pakistan would supply missile technology to other Muslim states. The MTCR is basically a suppliers club and places no restrictions on member states developing their own missile systems.[153]

All the above measures deal with reality of the Pakistan-India situation on the ground - with neither state having to renounce its defence capability

---

[150] Ibid

[151] Lodhi, op cit:12

[152] Ibid

[153] Ibid

even as mutual deterrence it strengthened. Until such times as the conflicts are resolved at least the two states will be refraining themselves from unrestrained and destabilising arms races - and will have moved from a cold war style, unstable relationship to a more stable, détente framework of interaction.

The goal of international efforts should now progressively turn to preventing further nuclear tests, persuading India and Pakistan to halt the production of fissile materials for nuclear explosives and taking other steps to head off a South Asian nuclear Arms Race, such as pressing both sides to curb their ballistic missile programmes.

Pakistan former Army chief greeting servicemen and PAF JF-17 Thunder multi-role combat aircraft.

INS Chakra, an Indian nuclear submarine leased from Russia.[154]

---

[154] https://en.wikipedia.org/wiki/Indian_Navy#/media/File:INS_Chakra.jpg

SAGHIR IQBAL

References

Afzal Mahmood, Mini-Starwars in Asia?, Dawn publishers Ltd, 1998

Air Forces Monthly - http://www.airforcesmonthly.com/

Anthony Davies, Will Iran Choose War?, Jane Defence Weekly, 23 September 1998

Anthony H.Cordesman, Western Strategic Interests and the India-Pakistan Military Balance, Ian Allan Ltd, 1988

Arnett, Nuclear stability and arms sales to India, Arms Control Today, 1997

Ashok Kapur, Pakistan's attitude to the NPT, Parchment Press, 1993

Aviation Industry Chengdu Aircraft Industry (Group) Co., Ltd. - http://cac.avic.com/web/

Aviation Industry Corporation of China, Ltd. (AVIC) - http://www.avic.com/en/index.shtml?PC=PC

AVIC - http://www.avic.com/en/forbusiness/militaryaviationanddefense/fighters/394351.shtml

B.H.Farmer, An Introduction to South Asia, Richard Clay & Co.Ltd, 1983

Brassey's, World Aircraft & Systems Directory, Brassey's Ltd, 1996

C. Philips, The nuclear Casebook, Polygon Books, 1983

CAC/PAC JF-17 Thunder - https://en.wikipedia.org/wiki/CAC/PAC_JF-17_Thunder

CATIC - http://www.catic.cn/front

Chapter Six: Asia, 2018, The Military Balance, vol. 118, no. 1, pp. 219

Chapter six: Asia. (2017). *The Military Balance, 117*(1), 237-350.

Chinese Military Aviation - http://chinese-military-aviation.blogspot.co.uk/

Chris Bishop, Encyclopedia of Air Warfare-Volume 2, Aerospace Publishing Ltd, 1997

Chris Taylor, Military Balance in Southeast Asia, House of Commons Library, 2011

Christopher Walker and Michael Evans, Pakistan Feared Israeli Raid, The Times, Wednesday June 3, 1998

Christopher Walker, Israel's Helped India for 20 years, The Times, Thursday June 4, 1998

Cindy Shiner, International Herald Tribune, 1998

Combat Aircraft.Com - http://www.combataircraft.com/en/Military-Aircraft/Fighter-Attack/

David Albright and Tom Zamora, India and Pakistan go Nuclear, Bulletin of Atomic Scientists, 1989

David Axe, War Is Boring - https://medium.com/war-is-boring/this-is-the-ultimate-mig-21-715bb9297261

Dawn Weekly, Kashmir Policy, Touch Media Co.Ltd, 1998

Defence Industry Daily, Pakistan & China's JF-17 Fighter Program - https://www.defenseindustrydaily.com/stuck-in-sichuan-pakistani-jf17-program-grounded-02984/

Defence.pk - https://defence.pk/

Dreamstime - https://www.dreamstime.com/

Edward W.Desmond, Unity or Chaos?, Time, November 12, 1990

Eric Arnett, Delhi able to play nuclear trump in game for control of Kashmir, The Times, May 1998

Eric Arnett, Military Capacity and the Risk of War-China, India, Pakistan and Iran, Oxford University Press, 1997

Eric Arnett, What Threat?, Bulletin of the Atomic Scientists, 1997

Fareed Zakaria, How to be a Great Cheap, NewsWeek, T.P.L Printers Ltd, May 25, 1998

Flickr - https://www.flickr.com/search/?text=jf-17%20thunder

Flight Global - https://www.flightglobal.com/news/articles/nigeria-to-acquire-three-jf-17-fighters-444709/

Flight International, Airforces of the World Directory, Marketforce Ltd, 1998

General Walter Walker, The Next Domino?, The Covenant Publishing Co.Ltd, 1980

Global Security - https://www.globalsecurity.org/

Government of Pakistan, Ministry of Defence - http://www.mod.gov.pk/

Hafeez Malik, Dilemmas of National Security and Co-operation, The Macmillan Press Ltd, 1993

Ibid

IISS, Strategic Survey 2011 – The Annual Review of World Affairs, Routledge, 2011

IISS, Strategic Survey 2012 – The Annual Review of World Affairs, Routledge, 2012

IISS, Strategic Survey 2013 – The Annual Review of World Affairs, Routledge, 2013

Impact International, Delhi Expands its Strategic Swath, News & Media Ltd, 1996

Imtiaz Bakhari, The beginning of another 'Great Game'?, Jang Publishers Ltd, September 26, 1998

Indian Air Force - http://indianairforce.nic.in/

Indian Navy - https://www.indiannavy.nic.in/

Indian Army - https://indianarmy.nic.in/index.aspx

India Today, Future Fire, 1998

India Today, Games of Brinkmanship, 1987

India Today, India and Pakistan hours away from a nuclear war, 1994

India Today, India is now a nuclear weapon state, Living India Media Ltd, May 1998

India Today, India is now a Nuclear Weapon State, Living Media India Ltd, 1998

India Today, Pakistan's nuclear test, what now, June 1998

Inter Services Public Relations (ISPR) - https://www.ispr.gov.pk/

International Institute for Strategic Studies (IISS), Military Balance 1998-99, Oxford University Press, 1998

J.A.S Greenville, History of the World, HarperCollins Publishers, 1994

J.Goldstein & J. Pevehouse, International Relations, United States, 2007

Jane Nolan, Ballistic Missiles in the Third World, Brookings Institutions, 1991

Janes 360 - http://www.janes.com/article/search?query=+JF-17

Janes Defence Weekly (JDW), On the Line of Fire, Janes Information Group Ltd, 1998

JDW, A Loss of Momentum, 1997

JDW, A Loss of Momentum, 1997

JDW, Asia's Missile Race Hots Up, 1994

JDW, Asia's Missile Race Hots Up, 1994

JDW, Country Survey- Pakistan, 1992

JDW, Country Survey-India, 1990

JDW, Country Survey-Pakistan, 1992

JDW, Fighting on the Roof of the World, 1998

JDW, IAF Follows up on Su-30 Offer, 1994

JDW, India and Pakistan move to prevent nuclear disaster, March 1999

JDW, India becomes Sixth Nuclear Weapons State, 1998

JDW, India Budget May Affect Modernisation, 1998

JDW, India's Search for a New SPG, 1994

JDW, Indian Budget Fall May Affect Modernisation, 1998

JDW, Latest Tests put India in Nuclear Arms Spotlight, 1998

JDW, Mounting Tensions in South Asia, 1996

JDW, Nuclear Submarine is being built in India, December 1994

JDW, Pakistan Needs up to 70 Nuclear Warheads, June 1998

JDW, Pakistan's Time for Reassessment, 1998

JDW, Trials Provide Data for Range of Weapons Yields, 1998

JDW, USA links Chinese ties to missile Exports, 1994

JDW, Will Iran Choose War?, 1998

JF-17 Thunder - http://www.jf-17.com/

Johann Mcgeary, India's Surprise Nuclear Tests, Time May 25, 1998

Justin Bronk, So how good is Pakistan's JF-17 fighter? - https://hushkit.net/2018/01/25/so-how-good-is-pakistans-jf-17-fighter-analysis-from-rusi-think-tanks-justin-bronk/

KLJ-7A China Electronics Branch 14 airborne active phased array fire control radar - http://www.fx361.com/page/2017/0315/1131775.shtml

Lawrence Freedman, Atlas of Global Strategy, Macmillan Press Ltd, 1985

Lawrence Freedman, National Pride sets the Sabre Rattling, Daily Mail, May 29, 1998

Mahnaz Ipahani, Pakistan: dimensions of insecurity, Brassey's, 1990

Malcolm Chalmers, Confidence-Building in South-East Asia, Westview Press, 1996

Malcolm Chalmers, Owen Greene and Xie Zhiqiong, Asia Pacific Security & The UN, University of Bradford, 1995

Maleeha Lodhi, Nuclear Risk reduction and Conflict-Resolution in South Asia, Jang Publications Ltd, 1998

Mark J. Valencia, Trouble Waters, The Bulletin of the Atomic Scientists, 1997

Martin Sieff and Yoel Cohen, Pakistan Feared Israel's Strike during Nuclear test, Jewish Chronical, June 5 1998

Military   Factory   - https://www.militaryfactory.com/aircraft/detail.asp?aircraft_id=758

Military-Today.com   -   http://www.military-today.com/aircraft/jf17_thunder.htm

Ministry of Defence Production (Government Of Pakistan) - http://www.modp.gov.pk/

 Ministry of Information Technology and Telecommunication (MoITT), Government of Pakistan - http://www.moit.gov.pk/

Mustaq Ali Khan, Pakistan Army Green Book, Ferozsons (Pvt) Ltd, 1990

News International, Advani's Nuclear Blackmail, August 10, 1998

News International, India will have to reclaim Azaad Kashmir says Defence Minister, Jang Publications Ltd, 1998

News International, Israel offers India AWACS for Airbases as Part of 'Common Threat Perception', Jang Publishers Ltd, April 18, 1995

News International, Nuclear arms not to be used: Nawaz, June 1998

Nick Bisley, Building Asia's Security, Routledge, 2009

Nils Bhinda, The Kashmir Conflict-1990, Earthscan Publication Ltd, 1994

Official Gateway To The Government Of Pakistan - http://www.pakistan.gov.pk/index.html

Pakistan Aeronautical Complex (PAC) - http://www.pac.org.pk/

Pakistan Air Force - http://www.paf.gov.pk/

Patrick Brogan, World Conflicts-Why and Where they are Happening, Bloomsbury Publishing Ltd, 1992

Paul Dibb, Towards a New Balance of Power in Asia, Adelphi Paper 295, Oxford University Press, 1995

Paul Rogers, Guide to Nuclear Weapons 1984-85, C.J.W Printers Ltd, 1984

Peter G. Tsourus, Changing Orders-The Evolution of the World's Armies, Arms and Armour Press, 1994

Pixabay - https://pixabay.com/en/photos/?q=military&image_type=&cat=&min_height=&min_width=&order=popular&pagi=2

Quwa Defence News & Analysis Group - https://quwa.org

Rahimullah Yusufzai, Taliban's Achilles Heels, Jang Publishers Ltd, November, 1998

Rockwell Collins - https://www.rockwellcollins.com

S.weibo.com - http://s.weibo.com/weibo/jf-17?topnav=1&wvr=6&b=1

Sean Kay, Global Security in the Twenty-First Century, Rowman & Littlefield Publishers, Inc, 2006

Senate Standing Committee on Defence and Defence Production - http://www.senatedefencecommittee.com.pk/

Sidney Bearman, Strategic Survey 1993-1994, Published by Brassey's for the IISS, 1994

SinoDefence.com (also known as "China Defence Today") - http://sinodefence.com/

Sohu FC-1 "Fierce Dragon" cockpit mystery - http://mil.sohu.com/20061102/n246145079_4.shtml

Stockholm International Peace Research Institute (SIPRI), World Military Expenditure Prices 1987-96, Oxford University Press, 1997

Sunday Telegraph, India Celebrates its Nuclear dream, May 1998

Tarun Basu, Selective Satellite Tracking of Missiles Alledged, India Abroad, 1997

The Daily Telegraph, Nuclear Blasts Puts Pakistan in Arms Race, 1998

The Diplomat - https://thediplomat.com/tag/jf-17-thunder/

The Economist, Asian Security, Published by the Economist Newspaper Ltd, 1996

The Military Balance, 01/2017, Volume 117, Issue 1

The News International, Armed to the Teeth, Jang Publishers Ltd, 1998

The Times, Pakistan Blasts into the Arms Race, Times Newspaper Ltd, 1998

Umer Farooq, Striking Consequences, Janes Defence Weekly, 2 September 1998

Venon Hewit, The New International Politics of South Asia, Manchester University Press, 1997

Walter Walker, The Next Domino?, The Covenant Publishing Ltd, 1980

Y. Ammar, The Kashmir Factor, Palestine Times, 9 October 1991

Yoel Cohen, India bomb test may affect Israel Relations, Jewish Cronicle, Publishers Jewish Chronical Newspaper Ltd, May 29, 1998

Zian Mian, No time to think, Jang Publishers Ltd, 1998

Index

Images in this book fall under the following categories

(a) public domain (applicable to most official photos released by the military/manufacturers)

(b) free for commercial use

(c) used with explicit permission from the owner (applicable to all images from private websites)

(d) assumed to fall under (a) or (b) (applicable to images in printed media where no image owner is identified)

<u>Recently released books (2018)</u>

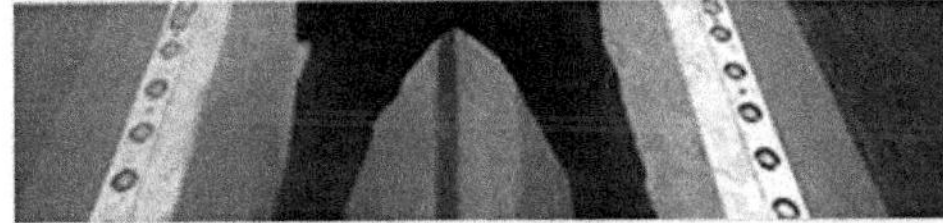

Major changes in East Asia have placed the region near the top of the World's strategic agenda. East Asia has until recently experienced the fastest regional economic growth rate in the world for many years. Economic co-operation has been flourishing and economic interests have become the major reason in reshaping East Asian international relations. However, there have also been changes in the security environment, due to many factors, such as the reduction of US forces in East Asia, the disintegration of the Soviet Union (the decline of the Soviet Union's presence in the region had led to renewed attention to traditional and potential rivalries among the major East Asian powers), and the concern of China's hegemonistic ambitions.

Product details

- **Paperback:** 106 pages
- **Publisher:** CreateSpace Independent Publishing Platform; 1 edition (16 Jan. 2018)
- **Language:** English
- **ISBN-10:** 1974062309
- **ISBN-13:** 978-1974062300
- **Product Dimensions:** 21.6 x 0.6 x 27.9 cm

The astronomical rising costs of modern combat has resulted in many countries being deprived of purchasing a modern combat aircraft and this has had an adverse effect on their security. Many nations have tried to undertake cost-effective measures for their defence needs.

Countries can either purchase very expensive modern aircraft or buy older aircraft that can be expensive to operate due to their high maintenance requirements. The Pakistan Air Force had initiated the plan to co-develop an affordable modern multi-role fighter aircraft with China. Chengdu Aircraft Corporation (CAC) in collaboration with Pakistan Aeronautical Complex (PAC, Kamra) have jointly developed the JF-17 Thunder combat aircraft (also known as the FC-1 Xiaolong Fierce Dragon in China).

JF-17 Thunder is a sophisticated light-weight multi-role, all weather, day/night fighter aircraft that is manufactured by Pakistan and China. The JF-17 Thunder has become a very cost-effective aircraft that costs very little compared to other modern aircraft. Many countries have shown an interest and a few have started to make orders. Some have described the JF-17 as the 'Ultimate MiG-21' arguing that the Chinese/Pakistani JF-17 builds on a classic warplane – although it has no resemblance and its level of sophistication is comparable to current advanced fighter aircraft on the market. This very modern and capable aircraft has the potential to become a potent platform that can serve with numerous air forces across the world. Product details

- **Paperback:** 178 pages
- **Publisher:** CreateSpace Independent Publishing Platform (26 Feb. 2018)
- **Language:** English
- **ISBN-10:** 1984055240
- **ISBN-13:** 978-1984055248
- **Product Dimensions:** 21.6 x 1.1 x 27.9 cm

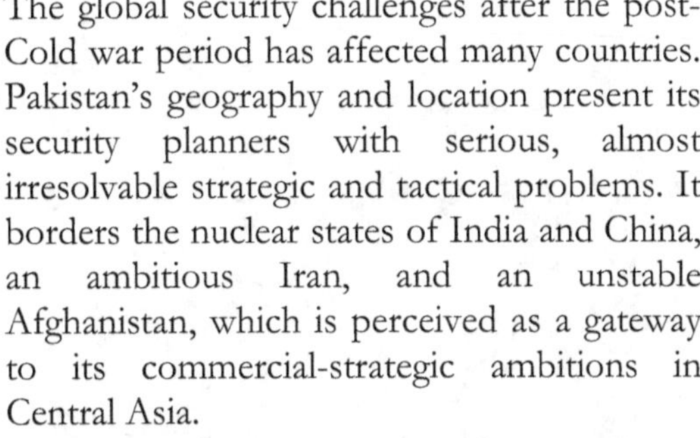

The global security challenges after the post-Cold war period has affected many countries. Pakistan's geography and location present its security planners with serious, almost irresolvable strategic and tactical problems. It borders the nuclear states of India and China, an ambitious Iran, and an unstable Afghanistan, which is perceived as a gateway to its commercial-strategic ambitions in Central Asia.

Pakistan's key security problems are a reflection of its history and domestic circumstances. The overriding concern of Pakistan is its internal and external security. Strategically, Pakistan lacks territorial depth. Its main cities and communication routes are relatively close to the border with India and are susceptible to attack. In addition, the headwaters of Pakistan's rivers and main irrigation systems originate from India. Pakistan's borders with India were also new and mainly unfortified and, in many places, were drawn in ways that made them indefensible. Because the borders were also un-demarcated, there was abundant chance for conflict. Pakistan has particularly been affected with a number of issues.

It has been argued by many that a Fourth generation/Hybrid war has been imposed on Pakistan, in order to break the nation (Balkanization of Pakistan into different parts) with the aim of making it either extremely weak or total destruction as a nation state (so that it is not able to challenge the hegemonistic ambitions of its adversaries).The purpose of this book is to assess the military security problems that Pakistan faces, and focus on its external security matters (military threats from neighbouring countries such as India, balance of power in the region, nuclear and ballistic missile threats, relationship with external powers, the high risk of war and its role on the 'War on Terror'), and its internal security problems (sectarianism, proliferation of small arms, refugees, ethnic violence, drug problem, economic weaknesses), and also its ability to cope with these problems.

Product details

- **Paperback:** 366 pages
- **Publisher:** CreateSpace Independent Publishing Platform; 1 edition (13 April 2018)
- **Language:** English
- **ISBN-10:** 1986169421
- **ISBN-13:** 978-1986169424
- **Product Dimensions:** 21.6 x 2.2 x 27.9 cm

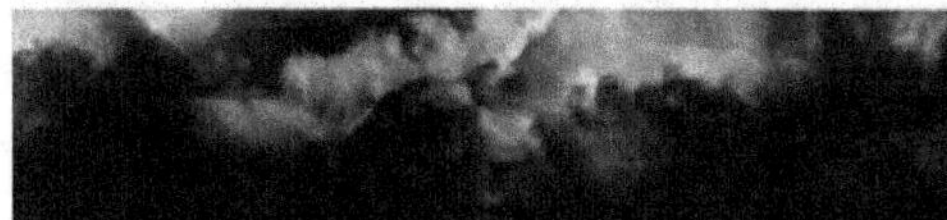

MISCALCULATION: RISKS OF INADVERTENT NUCLEAR WAR

SAGHIR IQBAL

An impending nuclear holocaust is likely to happen, if the world community does not take action. A conflict that has been simmering for many years is beginning to spiral out of control. Two nuclear powers have an unresolved dispute that has increased tensions in the region.

Both countries are purchasing and developing sophisticated state-of-the-art weapons that could unleash great terror and destruction on the populations of both countries – with also serious global ramifications.

The world's most dangerous flashpoint, has the highest chance of a nuclear war occurring – it is deemed by many to be more serious that the Cuban Missile Crisis and North Korea's nuclear sabre rattling. The dispute needs to be amicably resolved between both nations and confidence building measures need to be implemented.

Product details

- **Paperback:** 154 pages
- **Publisher:** CreateSpace Independent Publishing Platform; 1 edition (16 April 2018)
- **Language:** English
- **ISBN-10:** 1717040403
- **ISBN-13:** 978-1717040404
- **Product Dimensions:** 21.6 x 0.9 x 27.9 cm

Pakistan faces a number of threats from internal and external forces – with the aim of weakening the country and an attempt to 'balkanise' Pakistan in to different parts. The Pakistani Chief of Army, General Qamar Javed Bajwa has said that "a hybrid war had been imposed on Pakistan to internally weaken it, but noted that the enemies were failing to divide the country on the basis of ethnicity and other identities".

Furthermore he states, "Our enemies know that they cannot beat us fair and square and have thus subjected us to a cruel, evil and protracted hybrid war. They are trying to weaken our resolve by weakening us from within". Conflicts in Ukraine, Israel and Lebanon (Hizbullah), Syria, Libya, War on Terror in Afghanistan and its impact in Pakistan etc., have resulted in multi-layered efforts to destabilise a functioning state and polarize its society. The centre of gravity is to target population in hybrid warfare. The aim of the adversary is to influence influential policy makers and key decision makers by combining kinetic operations with subversive efforts. The aggressor often resorts to covert actions, to avoid attribution or retribution. At the moment there is no universally accepted definition of hybrid wars – the term is too abstract and is seen by some as using a fancy term to refer to irregular methods to counter conventionally stronger forces.

Accordingly, many say that the new definitions of 4th generation or hybrid wars are really the repackaging of the traditional clash between the armed forces of nation states and the non-state insurgents. This book will be assessing Pakistan's insecurity and the hybrid wars imposed onto it by its adversaries. It will look at a number of issues that Pakistan is facing (military imbalance, economic and political weaknesses, internal and external security threats and the impact of hybrid warfare on Pakistan).

Product details

- **Paperback:** 132 pages
- **Publisher:** CreateSpace Independent Publishing Platform; 1 edition (17 Jun. 2018)
- **Language:** English
- **ISBN-10:** 1721510095
- **ISBN-13:** 978-1721510092
- **Product Dimensions:** 21.6 x 0.8 x 27.9 cm

Each year billions of dollars' worth of arms are procured between various nations, despite the fact that many millions of people live in desperate poverty, many will die from hunger and hunger related diseases. Weapons of increasing firepower and the missiles to deliver them accurately are being acquired, mainly through the Global Arms Trade. This means that we must expect wars in the world to become increasingly violent and destructive.

This book focuses on what the arms trade is and its impact on the world, the wars which have resulted or were sustained by this trade. It is necessary to know which countries sell arms and which ones buy. Also it is important to have some idea of how large the trade is. The international trade in arms has considerably increased since World War 2. Major weapons (aircraft, missiles, tanks and ships) probably account for about one-half of the total trade in weapons and equipment. Many countries and their respective Military-Industrial Complex are 'making a killing' in the world's largest trade in the buying and selling of military technology (weapons).

Product details

- **Paperback:** 90 pages
- **Publisher:** CreateSpace Independent Publishing Platform (28 July 2018)
- **Language:** English
- **ISBN-10:** 1721773150
- **ISBN-13:** 978-1721773152
- **Product Dimensions:** 15.2 x 0.5 x 22.9 cm

The global security challenges since World War II and thereafter (post-Cold war period) has affected many countries. This has resulted in a number of countries pursuing a nuclear weapons programme to provide them with the ultimate security – the belief that the fear of utter annihilation of their opponents would result in deterrence and eventually detente. According to Kristensen and Norris (2014), there are approximately 16,300 nuclear weapons located at some 97 sites in 14 countries. Many of these weapons are in military arsenals (roughly 10,000), with the remaining ones being in the process of retirement and awaiting dismantlement. Accordingly, 93% of the total global inventory resides in Russia and the United States of America. The remaining weapon stockpiles are in the United Kingdom (UK), France, China, India, Pakistan, North Korea and Israel.

This book looks at the proliferation of weapons of mass destruction (WMD), the double standards and hypocrisy practiced by the five declared nuclear powers. It gives a brief short history of nuclear development in the nuclear countries and the impact of nuclear war. It argues that the only way to eradicate these horrendous weapons is for the five declared nuclear powers to make immediate measures to dismantle the weapons and stockpiles of weaponised materials – as they had agreed under the Nuclear Non-proliferation Treaty (NPT).

Product details

- **Paperback:** 146 pages
- **Publisher:** CreateSpace Independent Publishing Platform (31 July 2018)
- **Language:** English
- **ISBN-10:** 1983910414
- **ISBN-13:** 978-1983910418
- **Product Dimensions:** 15.2 x 0.8 x 22.9 cm

This book looks at the concept of 'terrorism' and its primary aim of creating a climate of fear. Any discussion of terrorism has to firstly define its terms: what do we mean by terrorism and how does it manifest itself in contemporary accounts and moreover, what is the difference between legitimate military action and one based on terror? The definitions of terrorism are complex and depend, to a very large extent, on who one is asking. A government defence adviser would, for instance, have a markedly different notion of what constitutes terrorism than a member of a paramilitary organisation and an ordinary member of the public might have a notion based somewhere on the interaction between these two depending on their socio-cultural background. This is primarily the main reason why the term has not been universally accepted by all scholars or academics.

There are many reasons why political groups attempt to bring about radical change through terrorism. People are often frustrated with their position in society. They may in some way feel persecuted or oppressed because of their race, religion, or they feel exploited by a government. Any group that uses terrorist actions have very complex and powerful reasons to engage in those activities. The usual experience of violence by a stronger party has historically turned victims into terrorists. State terror very often breeds collective terror. Because 'terrorism' is a word that has been used so much and so loosely that it has lost a clear meaning. It can be argued that terrorists are not born, but created as issues of today develop into the conflicts of tomorrow.

Product details

- **Paperback:** 202 pages
- **Publisher:** CreateSpace Independent Publishing Platform (7 Aug. 2018)
- **Language:** English
- **ISBN-10:** 1724714856
- **ISBN-13:** 978-1724714855
- **Product Dimensions:** 15.2 x 1.2 x 22.9 cm

When NATO was founded in 1949, it had a clearly defined role. The demise of the Cold War, the disintegration of the Soviet Union and the collapse of communism in the period from 1989 to 1991 called into question NATO's future role and its continued existence. The primary role was called into question over its future relevance in the post-Cold War world. The reason for NATO was essentially a military alliance to deter Soviet and Warsaw Pact aggression – however, once the threat had finished its role had been challenged by many academics and governments. Many analysts felt that NATO was nothing more than an out of date alliance from the Cold War with no real future. Others would say, however, that an organisation such as NATO was still crucial in the modern world to ensure that countries do not act unilaterally, but co-operate with allies. In view of the situations, NATO has managed to address new issues and adapt its roles on different levels.

- **Paperback:** 66 pages
- **Publisher:** CreateSpace Independent Publishing Platform (10 Aug. 2018)
- **Language:** English
- **ISBN-10:** 1725092816
- **ISBN-13:** 978-1725092815
- **Product Dimensions:** 15.2 x 0.4 x 22.9 cm

Tony Wilkinson was a small time crook and a thief - and not very successful

at that. He was called 'fate' by anybody who knew him due to these reasons. Because, it seemed, fate had dealt a nasty blow to his occupation, and to him. Because every job he ever pulled, backfired on him and had proved to be costly for him. Things were going to change after he made a plan to improve his situation. However, his plan came up with unexpected hurdles. He then looked at his past and fate asked the question to himself, "What chance did I stand against Kismet?"

- **Paperback:** 33 pages
- **Publisher:** Independently published (8 Dec. 2018)
- **Language:** English
- **ISBN-10:** 1790958296
- **ISBN-13:** 978-1790958290
- **Product Dimensions:** 15.2 x 0.2 x 22.9 cm

Peter Hyde was probably one of the finest yachtsmen in the world and was participating in the Schooner Silver Surf championship contest out of Auckland, in New Zealand.Peter and his crew were going to take a short cut to Tahiti when suddenly something exploded in the sea, a half mile from where they were. The explosion was just the beginning…..

- **Paperback:** 102 pages
- **Publisher:** Independently published (10 Dec. 2018)
- **Language:** English
- **ISBN-10:** 1791375162
- **ISBN-13:** 978-1791375164
- **Product Dimensions:** 15.2 x 0.7 x 22.9 cm

Israel had attempted to destroy the Kahuta plant as it had successfully destroyed the Iraqi nuclear plant in Osirak. It needed Indian help in undertaking this mission. There were strong ties between the Israeli Mossad and Indian RAW intelligence agencies. An Indo-Israeli joint plan was initiated. Both countries had felt that it was in their interest to undergo a preventive strike on Pakistani nuclear facility in Kahuta.

- **Paperback:** 68 pages
- **Publisher:** Independently published (16 Dec. 2018)
- **Language:** English
- **ISBN-10:** 1791811035
- **ISBN-13:** 978-1791811037
- **Product Dimensions:** 15.2 x 0.4 x 22.9 cm

ABOUT THE AUTHOR

Saghir Iqbal is a researcher in International Relations and Security Studies. He is an experienced Intelligence Analyst and has achieved a number of qualifications in this field. He is also a Lecturer in Business Management as well as an Examiner for A Level History and Business. Saghir Iqbal has a subject specialism in the following areas:

International Politics of the Cold War 1945-1991
Conflict Resolution in International Society+
Global and North-South Security Studies
Britain in the World
Disarmament Processes: History and Theory
Nationalism and Ethnicity in Post-Cold War Politics
Middle East: Area in Conflict
European Security
International Politics of the Environment
The United Nations, Peacekeeping and Intervention
Disarmament Processes: Current Problems
Globalisation and the South
International Terrorism
International Politics and Security Studies
Introduction to Peace Studies
Politics of the Global Environment
Regional Security in East Asia
Critical Security studies

Recently released books (2018)

- Dangerous Flashpoints in East Asia: The Military Build-up
- JF-17 Thunder: The Making of a Modern Cost- effective Multi-role Combat Aircraft
- Pakistan's War Machine: An Encyclopedia of its Weapons, Strategy and Military Security
- Miscalculation: Risks of Inadvertent Nuclear War
- Hybrid Warfare and its Impact on Pakistan's Security
- Making a Killing: The Scourge of the Global Arms Trade
- Nuclear Apartheid: Bullying, Hypocrisy and the Double Standards on Nuclear Weapons
- Terrorism: Creating a Climate of Fear

Website: www.saghir.co.uk